FELLOWSHIP

OF

I0617082

GOSPEL

CRUSADERS

INTERNATIONAL

All At It – Always At It - Everywhere At It

And daily...they ceased not to teach and preach *Jesus Christ.*
Acts 5:42

Dr. Tom Sexton

GOSPEL CRUSADERS

Training

"And he gave some, apostles; and some, prophets; and some, evangelists; and some, pastors and teachers.

For the perfecting of the saints, for the work of the ministry, for the edifying of the body of Christ:

Till we all come in the unity of the faith, and of the knowledge of the Son of God, unto a perfect man, unto the measure of the stature of the fulness of Christ." Ephesians 4:11-13.

"Trained workers are a churches greatest asset."
Lee Roberson

Dr. Tom Sexton

www.FiveStarChristianMinistries.com

Content

My Time With Dr. Lee Roberson

By Dr. Tom Sexton

"Everything Rises And Falls On Leadership" Dr. Lee Roberson

My wife Nancy and I, along with our two small children, moved to Chattanooga, Tennessee in the late 1970's. We joined Highland Park Baptist Church, and I enrolled in Tennessee Temple Bible School.

At that time, under Dr. Roberson's leadership, the Highland Park Baptist Church, according to the "Chattanooga Times" was the largest Baptist Church in the world with a membership of 40,000. There would be 8,000 and upwards of 10,000 in Sunday school, on special days. The church had hundreds of trained workers. Laypeople headed up every ministry of that great church.

Highland Park Baptist Church

Midweek Prayer Meeting

Chattanooga TN 1981

While I was a student, my wife and I worked in the bus ministry, the Sunday school, and all the visitation programs of the church. Every week we faithfully served in our place of service. God blessed the ministries we were in, and we were even given an opportunity to start a new division of the Sunday school.

4

After graduation, Dr. Roberson asked me to join the staff of the church as the Bus Director, and the Director of the Afternoon Sunday School. We had 65 Sunday school buses which brought boys, girls, teens, and adults to Sunday school every week. I was Dr. Roberson's last Assistant to the Pastor, and he ordained me into the ministry.

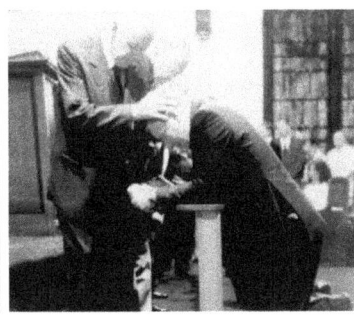

At that time, many of the men and women, who had stood with Dr. Roberson for years, which made up the workforce of that great church, had gone to Heaven. Dr. Roberson was faced with the great challenge of training a new generation of laypeople to help him carry on what God had put in his heart to do.

He gave me the opportunity to train and equip all the new laypeople who would be joining the workforce. I met with either Dr. Roberson or Dr. Faulkner every week and learned directly from them how they trained the workers and leaders in that great ministry.

I learned from Dr. Roberson himself about what truth needed to be in the hearts of people to help them be in the spirit of one accord, to work together, and carry-on God's plan for the ages. What I gleaned from him turned out to be the greatest education and training any young man could ever receive.

Dr. Roberson believed the work of the Lord was not just for a chosen few, but for every believer in the pew. He put the Lord's work in the hands of the laypeople, and they filled their Jerusalem with the Gospel. Allowing laypeople to serve at the highest levels of leadership, in the church, was the secret of Dr. Roberson's success. He would often say, "Trained workers are a churches greatest asset."

Dr. Roberson, my beloved pastor, helped me understand that what the Lord wants done in this world can be found in the hearts of His people, and that our ministry is to help them do what God has put in their hearts to do. Under his ministry, I gave my life to help believer's do what God has put in their hearts to do.

The will of God for my life, is to help people do the will of God with their life. My heart's desire for all believers is to have a good day at the Judgement Seat of Christ.

God gave me a measure of understanding to see the structure of leadership, in that great church, and how to teach and train the next generation of believers. What I learned from him is what I have tried to invest in the next generation of believers around the world.

Over the years I have taken what I learned from the life and ministry of Dr. Roberson and the great laypeople that I have known, and taught children, teens, men, women, church leaders, missionaries, evangelists, and pastors around the world.

Five Star Christian Ministries is what I learned from Dr. Roberson about building believers at every level of Christian service. This book, "Training Gospel Crusaders," is a small sample of what I gleaned from my mentors.

I believe the greatest need in our churches today are trained workers, both men and women., and spiritual leadership.

The three most difficult things to do in the Christian life are:

"Keep your life right with God and man."

"Stay on track with God's plan for your life."

"Be excited and encouraged with what God has given you to do."

Because, "Everything Rises And Falls On Leadership" Dr. Lee Roberson

Introduction

Dr. Lee Roberson, my dear beloved pastor said, "Trained workers are a churches best asset." It takes time and commitment to train workers and leaders in the Lord's work. We must be determined to train and equip the next generation of the Lord's army, if we are going to continue the mission Christ gave us and take the Gospel to the ends of the earth.

The Bible says, "And he gave some, apostles; and some, prophets; and some, evangelists; and some, pastors and teachers; For the perfecting of the saints, for the work of the ministry, for the edifying of the body of Christ: Till we all come in the unity of the faith, and of the knowledge of the Son of God, unto a perfect man, unto the measure of the stature of the fulness of Christ." Ephesians 4:11-13.

The generation who trained me believed the Lord's work was not just for a chosen few, but for every believer in the pew.

There is a job for all believers. The Bible says, "For we must all appear before the judgment seat of Christ; that everyone may receive the things done in his body, according to that he hath done, whether it be good or bad." II Corinthians 5:10.

"Every man's work shall be made manifest: for the day shall declare it, because it shall be revealed by fire; and the fire shall try every man's work of what sort it is." I Corinthians 3:13.

These verses teach us that every believer will stand before the Lord Jesus and give an account of the work God had for them to do. Since every believer will have this meeting one day, then every believer has something that their life is responsible to do.

There is no getting out of this appointment with God. The following lessons have been put together for the purpose of training men and women in world evangelism through the local church.

May the Lord Jesus use these lessons and His people to reach the world with the Gospel. May God richly bless all who use them. Dr. Tom Sexton, John 8:29.

Our Threefold Purpose

"Go ye into all the world and preach the gospel to every creature."
Mark 16:15

Publish the Gospel among all nations.

Jesus said, "And the gospel must first be published among all nations." Mark 13:10. Gospel Crusaders say with faithfulness and conviction, "I am not ashamed of the gospel of Christ: for it is the power of God unto salvation to everyone that believeth; to the Jew first, and also to the Greek." Romans 1:16.

We are to make sure no one is left out. Our goal is to "preach the gospel to every creature." Jesus said, "But ye shall receive power, after that the Holy Ghost is come upon you: and ye shall be witnesses unto me both in Jerusalem, and in all Judaea, and in Samaria, and unto the uttermost part of the earth." Acts 1:8.

Five Star Christian Ministries provides Gospel tracts in many languages, to make sure everyone can hear the Gospel in their language. They are printed in a way which allows them to be displayed in churches, schools, businesses, and a host of other places. Some "Gospel Crusaders" have what we call, "Gospel Tract Routes" where they replenish tracts regularly.

Bring the next generation of believers forward in the Christian faith.

Paul said to all who are followers of Christ, "But continue thou in the things which thou hast learned and hast been assured of, knowing of whom thou hast learned them;" II Timothy 3:14.

The Word of God gives light to all who learn its truths and follow the teachings of Jesus. It is these truths, learned from the Bible, which build Christian character and convictions in a believer's life.

This wisdom and understanding from God, which we call the ABCs of Jesus, completes the circle of education in one's life, allowing believers to use the knowledge gained in their years of living.

We must do all that is in our power to help the next generation of believers continue in the faith we have been entrusted with.

Paul said, "And the things that thou hast heard of me among many witnesses, the same commit thou to faithful men, who shall be able to teach others also." II Timothy 2:2.

Encourage one another.

The Bible says, "But exhort one another daily, while it is called To day; lest any of you be hardened through the deceitfulness of sin." Hebrews 3:13.

We believe it is one of the "daily" duties of every believer to encourage one another in the Lord. In other words, God wants you to encourage someone every day. So, "let us consider one another to provoke unto love and to good works: Not forsaking the assembling of ourselves together, as the manner of some is but exhorting one another: and so much the more, as ye see the day approaching." Hebrews 10:24-25.

As a member of the 'Fellowship of Gospel Crusaders," we agree to do our part in encouraging one another.

These three simple, yet powerful truths, unite all who are joined together in the "Fellowship of Gospel Crusaders" worldwide.

The world is waiting on the Gospel. May God's richest blessings be upon you.

"All at it. Always at it."
JPM

Do We Have What It Takes?

"Through wisdom is a house builded; and by understanding it is established: And by knowledge shall the chambers be filled with all precious and pleasant riches." Proverbs 24:3-4.

Three words in our text helps us to know what God is looking for in the people He uses to accomplish His work. He looks for people with knowledge, wisdom and understanding. Do we have what God is looking for? Do we have what it takes to continue the mission God has given us? My beloved pastor, Dr. Lee Roberson, was one such man. He often said, "Everything rises and falls on leadership."

I learned from him that a leader is not someone who lords over people or controls their every move; but is someone who accepts responsibility for the mission God has given them, and also is someone who is willing to let other believers use their gifts and abilities to help them.

One of the great truths I learned from Dr. Roberson was to believe that every Christian we meet can have a part in what the Lord Jesus has given us to do. We must find a way for all of Gods people to invest their lives in the Lord's work. Every church member is not a bullseye Christian, but every child of God can, at some level, have a part in God's plan for the ages.

We need men and women with "knowledge."

First, they must know God. Paul said, "That I may know Him, and the power of His resurrection," Philippians 3:10. Do you know the Lord Jesus as your personal "Saviour?" This is where we all must begin.

Second, they must know God's Word. The Bible says, "My people are destroyed for lack of knowledge" Hosea 4:6. We need to have a firm grip on God's Word and God's Word needs to have a firm grip on us.

Third, they must know the challenges they are facing. The Bible says, "the children of Issachar, ...which were men that had understanding of the times, to know what Israel ought to do." I Chronicles 12:32. God is looking for believers who know what is going on. He wants us to see the big picture.

We need men and women with "wisdom."

"Wisdom" is the ability to work with people who have "knowledge." I used to think that what believers needed were "people skills" to work with other people, but now I know that "people skills" is not Biblical. God's people need "wisdom."

One thing God tells us about Moses is, "Moses was learned in all the wisdom..." Acts 7:22. In other words, he knew how to work with people, all people. The good news is, "If any of you lack wisdom, let him ask of God," James 1:5.

We need men and women with "understanding."

"Understanding" is seeing the big picture of what God is doing and seeing how it all works together with the resources available. "Knowledge" is not enough. You must know Jesus and His Word. "Wisdom" is not enough. We must put "knowledge" to work.

Believers who have "understanding" of the times we live in, and "knowledge" of what needs done, will be given the "wisdom" to work with people.

Paul prayed for the believers in the church at Ephesus to receive, "knowledge, wisdom, and understanding." Ephesians 1:17-18.

"People must have some intrinsic worth, or God would not care so tenderly for them, they increase in value after they are saved."

JPM

The Great Commission

Jesus said, "Go ye therefore, and teach all nations, baptizing them in the name of the Father, and of the Son, and of the Holy Ghost: teaching them to observe all things whatsoever I have commanded you: and, lo, I am with you alway, even unto the end of the world. Amen." Matthew 28:18-20.

According to God's plan we are to **G**o after people, **T**ell them how to be saved, **B**aptize them and **T**each them how to live the Christian life. The Great Commission is our mission from God. God has a plan to reach the world, and it works <u>if</u> we will do it.

Jesus said, "...I will build my church..." Matthew 16:18. I believe if we follow the plan God has given to us, it will work in the day we live. What makes a great church? Remember, God measures a church by the sort, not necessarily by the size. Our work is going to be rewarded for what "sort" it is. The Bible says, "...the fire shall try every man's work of what <u>sort</u> it is." I Corinthians 3:13. Here are four ingredients in every great church, no matter the size:

1.**Great churches** have people who have compassion, and who genuinely care about others.

2. **Great churches** have people who are winning personal victories.

3.**Great churches** have people who have the joy of the Lord.

4.**Great churches** have people who are growing in the knowledge of our blessed Saviour.

These four ingredients can be found in every great church, and they are the result of doing the four things Christ has commanded us to do. **G**o after people, **T**ell them how to be saved, **B**aptize them, and **T**each them how to live the Christian life. They are the result of obeying His command.

As We Go, God Gives Us Compassion

Great churches have people who have compassion and a love for others. The Bible says, "Go ye therefore..."

As we go, God does something in our lives. He gives us compassion. The Bible says, "And Jesus went about all the cities and villages, teaching in their synagogues, and preaching the gospel of the kingdom, and healing every sickness and every disease among the people. But when he saw the multitudes, he was moved with compassion on them..." Matthew 9:35-38.

As we see the need of people, God changes how we see them. He gives us compassion for people. God puts the people we see in our hearts. Paul said about the people he ministered to, "I thank my God upon every remembrance of you...because I have you in my heart..." Philippians 1:3,7.

When our heart is filled with people, we become more like Jesus. The secret to having compassion is to go. God will give us the laborers to reach the people we have in our heart. Jesus said, "Pray ye therefore the Lord of the harvest, that he will send forth labourers." Matthew 9:38. Would Jesus ask us to pray for a need He could not meet? Here is the way it works. As we pray, God looks in our heart. The Bible teaches us, "the LORD seeth not as man seeth; for man looketh on the outward appearance, but the LORD looketh on the heart." I Samuel 16:7.

God sees our hearts desire and gives us what we need to accomplish it. He knows if we truly have people in our hearts. God will only give us what we need to accomplish what we have in our hearts to do.

As We Share the Gospel, God Gives Us Victory

Great churches have people who win personal victories. The Bible says, "Go ye therefore and teach all nations...and, lo, I am with you." It is when we tell people how to be saved, we win personal victories. God has promised us His presence as we go, and it is in His presence we win every victory.

How do we get a Christian into the presence of God? By getting them to tell others how to be saved. The Bible says, "But ye shall receive power, after that the Holy Ghost comes upon you: and ye shall be witnesses unto me." Acts 1:8. We once talked often about God's power in our lives, and about being filled with the Holy Spirit, but now it is rarely mentioned from our pulpits.

I asked Dr. Roberson, "How can you tell if somebody is filled with the Holy Spirit?" He said, "It is easier to tell if they are not filled. If they are not filled with the Holy Spirit," he said, "they are restless, discontented, and have no fruit."

Are you restless, discontented and void of fruit? Start telling people how to know the Lord as their personal Saviour and you will start winning some victories. Encourage new Christians to give out gospel tracts and to tell people why Jesus died, and you will see them also win many personal victories.

When We Surrender, God Gives Us Joy

Great churches have people who have the joy of the Lord. The joy of the Lord is a result of a surrendered life. The Christian life can be summed up in one word, **Surrender.**

The Bible says, "The joy of the Lord is your strength." Nehemiah 8:10. Joy is so important in the Christian's life, that if we do not have it, we should pretend we have it until we get the real thing. Joy is a result of a surrendered life. That is why, in the Bible, we find people getting saved and baptized the same day. The Bible says, "Then they that gladly received His word were baptized: and the same day." Acts 2:41.

Some believe that people should not be baptized until they understand salvation. I have a ring on my finger, a wedding band. It means that I am married. Let us pretend I said, "I am not going to wear this ring until after I understand what it means to be married." I am a great Grandfather, and I am still trying to figure out what it means to be married. People should be baptized because Jesus wants them to be baptized. God knows that when people obey Christ Jesus, they get the joy of the Lord.

As We Teach Others, We Grow

Great churches have people who are growing in the Lord. Christians grow in the Lord by teaching others how to live for Christ. The Bible says we are to teach the next generation of believers "all things." As we teach the Word of God to others, we also grow in Christ.
We must believe that there is a job for every child of God. When I was

on staff at Highland Park, Dr. J. R. Faulkner came to my office and put a sign right in front of my desk. The sign said, "Think of ways to put others to work for Jesus." Think of ways and find something for everybody to do. Give people responsibility in the Lord's work, and they will grow in the Lord.

"The Bible is a personal letter from God to His family on earth. There is a lesson in it for all in every situation of life."

"We forget that we are stewards of the wisdom we have acquired as well as the money and other talents.

It is not the amount of work that tells, but work done through the power of the Holy Spirit."

JPM

Keeping the Gospel, the Main Thing

Jesus said, "And the gospel must <u>first</u> be published among all nations…. And he said unto them, Go ye into all the world, and preach the gospel to every creature." Mark 13:10,16:15.

What is the main thing? According to our Lord Jesus, the main thing is the one He put first. The main thing is to make sure the Gospel goes first. In other words, we begin by giving the Gospel to everyone. I am going to say something that may make you think I have lost my mind, but please hear me out. The world is not waiting to receive a Bible, or to have a Bible study. The world is waiting on the Gospel. If we give the Gospel first, we are keeping the main thing the main thing.

I have learned, in my mission work abroad, how important it is to give Gospel tracks to lost people; then to give Bible helps to new Christians, and to give Bibles to church members, so they can grow in the Lord. It is important to follow this order. Give Gospel tracts first, helps for new believers second, and then give Bibles to church members so they can grow in their newfound faith. Giving a Bible to a lost man is like giving the keys to a drugstore to a sick and dying man. If he can find in the drugstore, what will save him, he will live. But more than likely he will die with the keys to the drugstore in his pocket.

I. What is the Gospel?

Paul said, "I declare unto you the gospel which I preached unto you, which also ye have received, and wherein ye stand…how that Christ died for our sins…He was buried, and…He rose again the third day according to the scriptures." I Corinthians 15:1-4. The Gospel is the most important message in the Bible. Have you heard and believed the Gospel? The Gospel is the Death, Burial, and the Resurrection of Christ.

1. Christ died for our sins.
2. He was buried.
3. He rose again on the third day.

II. When should we give the Gospel?

Paul reminded the church in Corinth that he began his ministry with them by declaring the Gospel. "And I, brethren, when I came to you, came not with excellency of speech or of wisdom, declaring unto you the testimony of God. For I determined not to know anything among you, save Jesus Christ, and him crucified." I Corinthians 2:1-2.

We need a "Gospel First "movement in our churches. If we do not lead with the Gospel, we may never get around to giving it to people. Carrying Gospel tracts, on your person, helps all believers put the Gospel first in their new relationships. When we first meet people, we should give them a Gospel tract.

III. Why should the Gospel be first?

The Bible says, "How shall we escape, if we neglect so great salvation, which at the first began to be spoken by the Lord and was confirmed unto us by them that heard him." Hebrews 2:3. Think about the word "escape." We all understand how important it is to have an escape plan in life.

Exits are clearly marked in all buildings around the world. Flight attendants talk about the escape plan if an emergency takes place in flight. Passengers are told to turn around and find the exit. They want all passengers to pay attention to their instructions and make sure they see their exit.

The most important escape plan in the world is the Gospel. How shall **we** escape if we neglect so great salvation? God does not want anyone to die and burn. He wants people to use the "Door to Heaven" and escape. Jesus said, "I am the door." John 10:9. Jesus is the exit door from this world and the ONLY entrance door into Heaven. He said, "I am the way, the truth, and the life: no man cometh unto the Father, but by me." John 14:6.

There are many doors we walk through in life, but none are more important than the Door to Heaven. "For what shall it profit a man, if he shall gain the whole world, and lose his own soul? Or what shall a man give in exchange for his soul?" Mark 8:36-37. The Gospel <u>must</u> be first because it is the <u>only</u> way to Heaven from this world.

IV. How does the Gospel work?

"For I am not ashamed of the gospel of Christ: for <u>it is </u>the power of God unto salvation to everyone that believeth; to the Jew first, and also to the Greek." Romans 1:16.

The Gospel only works <u>if</u> we believe. It takes faith to believe, and faith comes by hearing the Word of God. The Bible says, "Faith cometh by hearing, and hearing by the word of God." Romans 10:17. What does a person need to believe to go to Heaven?

1. They must believe we are all sinners. "For all have sinned and come short of the glory of God." Romans 3:23.

2. They must believe sin must be paid for. "For the wages of sin is death; but the gift of God is eternal life through Jesus Christ our Lord." Romans 6:23.

3. They must believe Jesus paid our sin debt in full. "For he hath made him to be sin for us, who knew no sin; that we might be made the righteousness of God in him." II Corinthians 5:21.

4. They must receive Christ as their personal Saviour. "That if thou shalt confess with thy mouth the Lord Jesus, and shalt believe in thine heart that God hath raised him from the dead, thou shalt be saved." We also read, "For whosoever shall call upon the name of the Lord shall be saved." Romans 10:9 &13.

We must turn to Christ in repentance, and faith, believing the Gospel, and receiving Christ as our personal Saviour, if we want to be forgiven and go to Heaven when we die.

Paul said, "...I am not ashamed of the gospel of Christ: for it is the power of God unto salvation to everyone that believeth; to the Jew first, and also to the Greek." Romans 1:16.

Sharing the Gospel is something every Christian young person and adult can do. One does not have to be a seasoned saint to tell others what Jesus is doing in their life or to give them a Gospel tract.

Keeping The Main Thing,

The Main Thing

"The Gospel must first be published among all nations."

Jesus said this is Job "1" for all believers,

In every generation.

How sad so many are still waiting for us to obey.

Our obedience to Christ, could give to them

A glorious Crowning Day.

Eternal life is not achieved by following religious plans.

It is believing the Gospel,

Given by the One with nail prints in His hands.

There is much in life we all set out to do.

But along your life's journey, did doing

"The Main Thing," capture you?

Publishing the Gospel among every nation on earth,

Will only be done by those who understand a soul's worth.

When the lost, of all ages, stand before our great

Saviour and King.

Everyone will know then if we kept

"The Main Thing, The Main Thing.

New Steps In The Right Direction

"But if we walk in the light, as he is in the light, we have fellowship one with another, and the blood of Jesus Christ his Son cleanseth us from all sin." I John 1:7. Receiving Christ as your personal Saviour is the greatest decision of your life! These simple steps will help you in your newfound faith.

Step 1: Know That You Belong To Jesus

You have eternal life. "For God so loved the world, that He gave His only begotten Son, that whosoever believeth in Him should not perish, but have everlasting life." John 3:16.

You are a child of God. The Bible says, "But as many as received Him, to them gave He power to become the sons of God, even to them that believe on His name" John 1:12. God has a big family "...in heaven and earth..." And you are part of it. Ephesians 3:14-15.

You have a Heavenly Father Matthew 6:9 and brothers and sisters in Christ. The Lord Jesus said that He would never lose you. "...Of them which Thou gavest Me have I lost none" John 18:19.

Step 2: Be Baptized

"Then they that gladly received His word were baptized..." Acts 2:41.

"Therefore, we are buried with him by baptism into death: that like as Christ was raised up from the dead by the glory of the Father, even so we also should walk in newness of life" Romans 6:4.

Baptism identifies you with Christ, and you become part of a church. All Christians need a church home. You become a member by obeying Christ in believer's baptism.

Step 3: Share Your Newfound Faith With Family And Friends

Everyone who comes to Christ should become a Crusader for the Gospel. "Howbeit Jesus suffered him not, but saith unto him, Go home to thy friends, and tell them how great things the Lord hath done for thee, and hath had compassion on thee." Mark 5:19.

The Lord Jesus wants each of His children to be a witness. "But ye shall receive power, after that the Holy Ghost is come upon you: and ye shall be witnesses unto Me both in Jerusalem, and in all Judea, and in Samaria, and unto the uttermost part of the earth." Acts 1:8.

Step 4: Read Your Bible

"Thy word have I hid in mine heart, that I might not sin against Thee." Psalm 119:11.

The Bible is God's Instruction Book for us. Spend time in God's Word every day. "These were more noble than those in Thessalonica, in that they received the word with all readiness of mind, and searched the scriptures daily, whether those things were so." Acts 17:11.

What we do with the Bible determines what the Lord does with us.

Step 5: Be Faithful To Church

"Not forsaking the assembling of ourselves together, as the manner of some is; but exhorting one another: and so much the more, as ye see the day approaching." Hebrews 10:25.

Be a faithful Christian and get to know your brothers and sisters in the Lord. Determine to be a three-to-thrive Christian. Be faithful to Sunday morning services, Sunday night services, and midweek prayer meetings.

Step 6: Talk To God In Prayer

"Evening, and morning, and at noon, will I pray, and cry aloud: and He shall hear my voice." Psalms 55:17.

Talk to the Lord about your sin and failures. Talk to the Lord about your needs. Remember, God says that we "have not" because we "ask not." James 4:2.

Step 7: Grow As A Christian

"But grow in grace, and in the knowledge of our Lord and Saviour Jesus Christ. To Him be glory both now and forever, Amen." II Peter 3:18.

You have a new life, and you need to grow. Keep things out of your life that kill growth (Proverbs 6:16-19). Everyone that has this new life will grow.

Step 8: Tell Others How To Be Saved

"For I am not ashamed of the gospel of Christ: for it is the power of God unto salvation to everyone that believeth; to the Jew first, and also to the Greek." Romans 1:16.

People who know the Lord have a desire to tell others how to know Christ as their personal Saviour. Let your light shine. Telling others how to be saved is as simple as ABC.

"A" is for Admit. Admit that you are a sinner. "For all have sinned, and come short of the glory of God." Romans 3:23.

"B" is for Believe. Believe Jesus died for you. "But God commended His love toward us, in that, while we were yet sinners, Christ died for us." Romans 5:8.

"C" is for Call. Call upon the Lord Jesus Christ to save you. "For whosoever shall call upon the name of the Lord shall be saved." Romans 10:13.

These steps will help your life go in the right direction.

First Century Gospel Crusaders

"And it came to pass afterward, that He went throughout every city and village, preaching and shewing the glad tidings of the kingdom of God: and the twelve were with him, And certain women…and many others, which ministered unto him of their substance." Luke 8:1-3.

We have recorded in our text the Lord Jesus and the first Gospel Crusaders. The Bible says that He took these crusaders and went throughout every city and village in Galilee preaching the Gospel and "shewing the glad tidings of the kingdom of God."

It is amazing to read that the Lord took with Him so many people on this crusade. The disciples were with Him. These twelve men were still a work in progress. In the next chapter of Luke's Gospel, we read where they are reasoning among themselves who will be the greatest out of their group. This may be why Christ took with Him, on this crusade, "certain women…and many others."

This we know, the ones who were with Him, on this crusade, were people who had been saved by the grace of God and who were a living testimony that others could see. The Lord Jesus was not only "preaching" the Gospel, but He was "shewing" what the Gospel can do.

These dear folk had been totally transformed by the power of the Gospel. They were living proof that what Christ preached worked. The men, women, and I believe children, who traveled with Him to Galilee, did not learn how to serve God in a classroom, they learned by doing it. They were in the "Go with Jesus school." Which is the school all believers should be enrolled in.

Who Were These People?

"The twelve were with Him." The disciples were with Him. These are the men that He called into His work. They had been with him from the very beginning of His earthly ministry. We will learn more about these men in later messages but let me say for now that it is a sad commentary on believers of our day to know so little about the men Christ called out; men who changed the world. This may be one reason we see fewer young people answering the call of God today.

"Certain women" were with Him. Mary called Magdalene, Joanna, the wife of Chuza, and Susanna are the three women whose names are given to us. I like the fact that the Lord calls them "certain women." They are not called disciples, but they are a very important part of this crusade team. The Bible says that they had been "healed of evil spirits and infirmities."

They were following the Lord because they had been saved and set free from the power of darkness. These women loved the Lord, and they loved people and wanted to be a part of His work and ministry. We need more of these "certain women" and men who will join this mission from God.

"Many others, which ministered unto Him of their substance" were with Him. I am glad the Bible says that <u>many</u> others were with the Lord on this crusade. This helps us see that every child of God can become a Gospel Crusader. All can follow Jesus. The ones who are called, the people who have that certain place of service in their home church and "many others," which includes all believers, can be used of God if they become Gospel Crusaders. Are you going to be one of the "many others" who have found their place of service for the Lord?

How Did They Become Gospel Crusaders?

First, they "had been healed of evil spirits and infirmities." They heard and believed the Gospel, which is the power of God unto salvation. The Gospel brings new life to the one who believes. "If any man will come after me, let him deny himself, and take up his cross daily, and follow me." (Luke 9:23) They followed Christ in believer's baptism, and now they are following Him to Galilee.

If we want to follow the Lord, we must identify with Him, which is only done by denying ourselves, then taking up our cross and following Him. The first step, for many, is the most difficult step; denying to self.

What Did They Do On This Crusade?

First, they "went throughout every city and village…" showing what Christ had done for them. They were a living testimony of the grace of God. As I have said before, the only way that someone can truly understand the Gospel is to see a living testimony. A person can be saved by hearing and believing the Gospel, but when they see a living testimony, they understand what the Gospel can do in a person's life.

The Gospel truly is "the power of God unto salvation." Christians are "children of the <u>living</u> God" (Romans 9:26) "known and read of all men." (II Corinthians 3:20)

Second, they were willing to give to this cause "of their substance." Their giving made it possible. The Lord Jesus and all who traveled with Him were able to have this crusade because people gave. God did not drop money out of Heaven to pay for this crusade. The people who loved the Lord and the souls of men made it possible. They made an investment in the Gospel. How much do we value the work of the Lord? The people who lived in Jesus' day are no different than the people who live in our day.

People are people no matter when they live. They made an investment that is still clipping coupons in Heaven. I wrote a poem entitled "People Are People."

People Are People

People are just people, no matter the color of their skin.
At our best we are just people, flawed women, and men.
Naked we're born with so much to learn,
At the end of our journey naked we'll return.
Some make it big and others stay the same.
Some have great talent and achieve worldwide fame.
Some give their life to make all that they can.
Some come to Christ and faithfully follow His plan.
Some make fortunes and have the world in their hands.
Some lift up Jesus the Saviour for every man.
Millions who were in darkness have been given new birth,
By the ones taking the Gospel to the ends of the earth.
Yes, people are just people no matter when they live,
But the ones who count are the ones who give.

"Lay not up for yourselves treasures upon earth...But lay up for yourselves treasures in heaven."
Matthew 6:19-20

THE HEALING TOUCH OF GOD

The Bible says, "And it came to pass afterward, that he went throughout every city and village, preaching and shewing the glad tidings of the kingdom of God: and the twelve were with him, And certain women, <u>which had been healed of evil spirits and infirmities</u>..." Luke 8:1-3.

We read about those on the Lord's first century Gospel team, "<u>which had been healed</u> of evil spirits and infirmities." They had experienced the healing touch of God and were a living testimony of the power of the Gospel to save and deliver.

He wants His followers to have peace and forgiveness, and to live life with purpose. The Bible says, "He sent his word, and healed them, and delivered them from their destructions." Psalm 107:20. God says, "I am the LORD that healeth thee." Exodus 15:26. I believe in the healing touch of God. But how does God heal?

First, God Heals All Who Are Without Christ.

"And you hath he quickened, who were dead in trespasses and sins." Ephesians 2:1

This is the greatest healing of all. This is being brought from death unto life. This is when we are born again into the family of God. This is a healing that money cannot buy. In fact, this is a gift from God for all humanity. The most important healing that ever takes place in a person's life is this healing.

This healing changes everything about a person's life. The Bible says, "Therefore if any man be in Christ, he is a new creature: old things are passed away; behold, all things are become new." II Corinthians 5:17.

(If you do not know the Lord Jesus as your personal Savior, please turn to the chapter entitled "God Loves You," and read how you can know Him personally, <u>before</u> reading further.)

God Heals and Renews Our Minds

The wild man in Luke's Gospel was saved, "sitting at the feet of Jesus, clothed, and in <u>his right mind</u>." Luke 8:35.

In other words, salvation had completely transformed his thinking. He had the mind of the Lord. "Let this mind be in you, which was also in Christ Jesus:" Philippians 2:5.

This trophy, of Gods amazing grace, was now in his right mind. The thing that has our thought life will one day have us. The healing process of God, in a believer's life, begins with the healing of our mind.

Paul, in writing the believers in Rome said, "I beseech you therefore, brethren, by the mercies of God, that ye present your bodies a living sacrifice, holy, acceptable unto God, which is your reasonable service.

And be not conformed to this world: but be ye transformed by the <u>renewing of your mind</u>, that ye may prove what is that good, and acceptable, and perfect, will of God." Romans 12:1-2.

Only the Word of God, through the power of the Holy Spirit which indwells all believers, can renew a person's mind and thinking. Many come to Christ for salvation, but they never allow the Lord to renew their mind.

Without the mind of Christ, we will not be able to live the life God has planned for us. How sad to miss God's best for your life because you have never experienced this healing touch of God. Spend time in God's Word and let the Word of God change your thinking. Let the Bible become the final authority in your life.

God Heals and Purges Our Conscience

The Bible says, "How much more shall the blood of Christ, who through the eternal Spirit offered himself without spot to God, <u>purge your conscience from dead works</u> to serve the living God" Hebrews 9:14.

The healing touch of God purges our conscience when we meditate on the Word of God. God wants His children to live by faith and to have "a pure conscience." II Timothy 3:9. If we do not take the time to let God purge our conscience, we will one day be captured again. David said, "purge me." He asked the Lord to purge him of sin.

A "pure conscience" will keep you from accepting evil and help you to choose the right course in life. The Bible says, "It is not good to accept the person of the wicked, to overthrow the righteous in judgment." Proverbs 18:5. Remember, we all become and are captured by what we are willing to accept.

Before someone sins, they must first defile their conscience by accepting what they are about to do. You can hate what you do, you can ask forgiveness repeatedly, but until you have your conscience purged you will fall into the same trap repeatedly.

God Heals Our Wounded Spirit

The Bible says, "The spirit of a man will sustain his infirmity; but a wounded spirit who can bear," and "A merry heart doeth good like a medicine: but a broken spirit drieth the bones." Proverbs 17:22;18:14.

God blesses us and uses us because of our spirit. With our mind renewed, our thinking is changed, and our conscience purged, we are now able to have our wounded spirit healed. David was such a powerful man, but he had a wounded spirit. He needed the healing touch of God for his wounded spirit. He said, "Create in me a clean heart, O God; and renew a right spirit within me." Psalms 51:10.

God knows that the joy of the Lord is our strength, and we cannot have strength with a wounded spirit. The disciples ate their meat with "gladness." Acts 2:46.

God Heals Those Who Have A Broken Heart.

The Bible says, "He healeth the broken in heart, and bindeth up their wounds." Psalms 147:3.

Paul, in writing Timothy, reminded him of a man who broke his heart. He said, "Demas hath forsaken me, having loved this present world, and is departed unto Thessalonica..." II Timothy 4:10. Demas was a brother who was very close to Paul. Paul loved him. Demas will forever be known as the one who forsook Paul in the hour of need.

When Demas left, he discouraged others who were doing the work of the Lord. Sadly, many have lost their heart for the work of the Lord because of believers like Demas.

People will sometimes break your heart, and people with a broken heart have a tough time loving again. But what makes a child of God special is their love one for another. How do you love again? Put yourself back out there. Remember what makes people special is their ability to love and to be loved. You can love again! It is a risk to love people, but it is a risk we all must take.

God Heals Those Who Are Oppressed Of The Devil.

The Bible tells us, "How God anointed Jesus of Nazareth with the Holy Ghost and with power: who went about doing good, and healing all that were oppressed of the devil; for God was with him." Acts 10:38. The devil cannot possess a child of God.

The Bible says, "That Christ may dwell in your hearts by faith." Ephesians 3:17. If you have Christ in you, the devil cannot possess you. The Bible says, "...greater is he that is in you, than he that is in the world." I John 4:4.

The devil is not going to dethrone the Lord Jesus. You cannot be demon possessed if you are a child of God. However, the devil can oppress you.

What does it mean to be oppressed? It means to be convinced that you cannot go forward. The Bible says, "His own iniquities shall take the wicked himself, and he shall be holden with the cords of his sins." Proverbs 5:22.

The good news is that the Lord Jesus can heal all who are oppressed of the devil and help us take the next step in our journey with God. Jesus said, "The Spirit of the Lord *is* upon me, because he hath anointed me to preach the gospel to the poor; he hath sent me to heal the brokenhearted, to preach deliverance to the captives, and recovering of sight to the blind, to set at liberty them that are bruised." Luke 4:18.

"If the Son therefore shall make you free, ye shall be free indeed." John 8:36.

God Heals Families

Paul said to the Philippian jailer, who asked the most important question anyone could ask. He asked, "Sirs, what must I do to be saved? And they said, Believe on the Lord Jesus Christ, and thou shalt be saved, and thy house." Acts 16:30-31.

Notice they said, "believe...and thou shalt be saved, and thy house." God wants families to be together in Heaven. He wants every member of your family to know Him and be saved. No one who understands Gods eternal plan for man, would not want their family to spend eternity together with them in Heaven.

 My dear brother, who led me to Christ, said to me, "Heaven will not be Heaven for me if you are not there."

Paul had family members who were saved before he was saved. I am sure his saved family members knew of his hatred toward Christians and prayed earnestly for his salvation.

That is why he could say with conviction, "Thou shalt be saved and thy house" because he had family who were saved before he was saved.

Paul in writing the church in Rome said, "Salute Andronicus and Junia, my kinsmen, and my fellow prisoners, who are of note among the apostles, who also were in Christ before me." Roman 16:7. One of these was his sister who had a son that warned Paul of a plot to kill him. The Bible says, "And when Paul's sister's son heard of their lying-in wait, he went and entered into the castle and told Paul." Acts 23:16.

Never stop praying or give up on God saving your family. "The Lord is not slack concerning his promise, as some men count slackness; but is longsuffering to us-ward, not willing that any should perish, but that all should come to repentance." II Peter 3:9. He is not willing that your loved ones should perish.

God Heals Churches

The Bible says, "Wilt thou not revive us again: that thy people may rejoice in thee?" Psalms 85:6. Will our churches live again? The answer to that question is without a doubt the most important subject on the hearts and minds of God's people. Do you believe it is over and God's mission to reach the world ends with us? Are you ready to give up on advancing the Gospel at home and abroad?

What has happened to the church? According to the Lord Jesus we have left something very important behind us on our mission from Him. He said, "I have *somewhat* against thee, because thou hast left thy first love." Revelation 2:4. If we have left it behind us, we should go back and get it! Notice, three words Jesus said to the church. He said, "I know thy works, and thy labour, and thy patience..." Revelation 2:2.

A close look at the first century church helps us to understand what is missing in our day.

Paul, in writing the church in Thessalonica said, "Remembering without ceasing your work of faith, and labour of love, and patience of hope in our Lord Jesus Christ..." I Thessalonian 1:3.

We have "work" without faith, We have "labour" without love, and we have "patience" without hope. We have left behind our faith, our love, and our hope in our churches today. We need all three to have the healing touch of God in our churches.

God Heals Nations

God says, "If my people, which are called by my name, shall humble themselves, and pray, and seek my face, and turn from their wicked ways; then will I hear from heaven, and will forgive their sin, and will heal their land." II Chronicles 7:14.

Will God heal our nation? Our enemies, both at home and abroad all say, "NO." They believe America's best days are behind us. They say America's faith is dead.

They look at the empty buildings and say as Sanballat said in his day," Will they sacrifice? will they revive the stones out of the heaps of the rubbish which are burned?" Nehemiah 4:2. Are they correct? Will we live to see America come back to God?

The Bible says about Iseral when they were away from God, "Now for a long season Israel hath been without the true God, and without a teaching priest, and without law. But when they in their trouble did turn unto the LORD God of Israel, and sought him, he was found of them." II Chronicles 15: 3-4. For a long time, Israel had been living without God, "for a long season."

The Bible says about us, "That at that time ye were without Christ, being aliens from the commonwealth of Israel, and strangers from the covenants of promise, having no hope, and without God in the world:" Ephesians 2:12.

Most people today are living without God. They plan their lives without a thought of God. God does not enter their thinking, except in times of emergency. He has not been welcomed into their lives. The Israelites still believed in the existence of God, and they experienced and benefited from His providences, but even with all this they were "without the true God."

We are not told they were without a god, for everyone worships a god of some kind – the god of self, money, pleasure, or ambition. These words describe many people in our day. But when trouble came, they found God. They came back to God.

The Bible says, "But when they in their trouble did **turn** unto the LORD God of Israel, and **sought** him, He was **found** of them." In this verse there are three words which tell us how to find God, or, more correctly, how to be found of Him. We must:

TURN to Him from sin and from self. The Bible says we must be, "turned to God from idols to serve the living and true God." I Thessalonians 1:9.

SEEK the Lord and His pardon. The Bible says. "Seek ye the LORD while he may be found, call ye upon him while he is near." Isaiah 55:6.

FIND the true God. The Bible says, "if ye seek him, he will be found of you…He was found by them" II Chronicles 15:2,4. Have you found Him? God says, "I love them that love me; and those that seek me early shall find me." Proverbs 8:17.

God says, "I am the LORD that healeth thee." Exodus 15:26. We must have faith in the healing touch of God. Then an understanding that He begins with the saving of our soul and continues His healing touch all the way to the healing of our nation.

"Have faith in God" Mark 11:22

Are We Trustworthy?

The Bible says, "Trust in him at all times; ye people, pour out your heart before him: God is a refuge for us. Selah." Psalms 62:8.

The Lord Jesus can always be trusted with our life and our future because He always gives us the truth. Jesus said, "I am the way, the truth, and the life....and ye shall know the truth, and the truth shall make you free...if the Son therefore shall make you free, ye shall be free indeed." John 14:6; 8:32,36. We trust Jesus because of "the truth" He gives makes us free.

However, this is not the case with many we have in leadership in all areas of our lives. In our beloved nation it is getting increasingly difficult to find people, in government, who will just tell the truth. Sadly, this is also becoming a problem in the Lord's work.

One of the greatest challenges we face in our day is trusting our leaders in every area of life. Can we trust our leaders in government, in the medical profession, in our educational system, in business, and yes even in our churches? Reasonable people believe that if their leadership cannot be trusted by giving them the truth, they should not be trusted with their future. People in leadership must always give their followers the truth and nothing but the truth. This is certainly true in the ministry.

The Bible teaches that, "evil men and seducers shall wax worse and worse, deceiving, and being deceived." II Timothy 3:13. What people, who are deceiving others, do not understand is when they are deceiving others, they are really deceiving themselves. Their life will not end well.

The Bible says, "Better is the end of a thing than the beginning thereof." Ecclesiastes 7:8. Liars and deceivers will not have a good ending. One reason is their followers turn on them in the end. Another reason is no one wants to hear what they have to say or teach the next generation. If you are not trustworthy you will discover:

1. Family will stop following you. I Thessalonians 1:6. "And ye became followers of us, and of the Lord, having received the word in much affliction, with joy of the Holy Ghost:"

2. People you lead will not trust you with their future. II Timothy 3:14. "But continue thou in the things which thou hast learned and hast been assured of, knowing of whom thou hast learned them:"

3. Faithful Christians will not want to hear what you have been commissioned to teach them. II Timothy 2:2. "And the things that thou hast heard of me among many witnesses, the same commit thou to faithful men, who shall be able to teach others also."

4. You will not have a good ending in the mission and ministry God gave you. "I have fought a good fight, I have finished my course, I have kept the faith: Henceforth there is laid up for me a crown of righteousness, which the Lord, the righteous judge, shall give me at that day: and not to me only, but unto all them also that love his appearing." II Timothy 4:7-8.

5. If you are a child of God, you will not have a good day at the Judgement seat of Christ. "For we must all appear before the judgment seat of Christ; that everyone may receive the things done in his body, according to that he hath done, whether it be good or bad." II Corinthians 5:10.

"To be put in trust with the Gospel is a great trust.

There is no power strong enough to reform human lives but the power of the Gospel of the Son of God."

JPM

Examine Yourselves

"Examine yourselves, whether ye be in the faith; prove your own selves. Know ye not your own selves, how that Jesus Christ is in you, except ye be reprobates?" II Corinthians 13:5. Do you have the birth marks of a child of God? God has given us a portion of the Word of God for the purpose of examining ourselves to see if we are in His family.

The Bible says, "These things have I written unto you that believe on the name of the Son of God; that ye may know that ye have eternal life, and that ye may believe on the name of the Son of God." I John 5:13.

How important is having assurance of your salvation? I have learned, by working with people for forty years, that the reason most believers do not share their faith with others is because of doubt. Doubt will keep you from becoming a bold witness. Doubt will keep you from becoming a Gospel Crusader. If you doubt your salvation, how are you going to tell others how to know the Lord?

The good news is that **all** doubt concerning our salvation can be removed. The Bible says, "These things have I written unto you that believe...that ye may **know** that ye **have** eternal life." So, how can you know that you know Christ as your personal Saviour? How can **your** doubts be removed?

What if you were saved many years ago and you cannot remember all the details concerning your conversion, can you remove the doubt? Yes!

Take this simple test from God's Word and have the assurance you need to go forward for the Lord. The Bible says, "Examine yourselves, whether ye be in the faith." Prove your own selves and know "that Jesus Christ is in you..." II Corinthians 13:5. Here are four areas to examine in your life.

First, Christians Should Have A Desire To Do God's Will.

"And hereby we do know that we know Him, if we keep His commandments." I John 2:3.

A child of God has a new desire. The Bible says, "all things are become new" when we become Christians II Corinthians 5:17. All things truly mean all things. There is a difference between what a child of God desires and what the devil's crowd desires. The Lord Jesus said, concerning the devil's crowd, "Ye are of your father the devil, and the lusts of your father ye will do..." John 8:44.

Do you want to read the Bible? Do you want to pray? Do you want to be around God's people? Do you want others to know more about Christ? Christians may not always do right, but they have a desire to please the Lord. What is in your heart: to do God's will or to do the lust of the devil? If the answer is yes, I want to do God's will, check the box.

☐ I want to do God's will with my life and tell others how to know Him.

Second, Christians Should Love God's People.

"We know that we have passed from death unto life because we love the brethren. He that loveth not his brother abideth in death." I John 3:14.

This does not mean that you get along with all of God's people. The Lord has a big family. Anyone who has been part of a big family knows that there are times when family members have problems with each other. Families should love one another and want God's best for each other.

God wants His family to love each other and to be in a spirit of one accord. Who are the people you call friends? Are they believers or non-believers? Who do you enjoy spending time with? Do you love God's people? If the answer is yes, check the box.

☐ I love God's family and want to fellowship with them.

Third, Christians Should Experience Conviction When They Sin.

"Hereby know we that we dwell in Him, and He in us, because He hath given us of His Spirit." I John 4:13.

Does Christ live in you? Does His Spirit bear witness with your spirit? Does the Spirit of God convict you when you sin? I sometimes say to Christians, "You cannot live like a devil and sleep like a baby if you are a child of God." It is true! God promised that He will chasten His children. If you are without chastening, then you are not His child Hebrews 12:7-8. God also promises that He will lead His children. "For as many as are led by the Spirit of God, they are the sons of God" Romans 8:14. If you can say that this is true in your life, check the box.

☐ I am convicted by the Holy Spirit and have experienced the leading of the Spirit.

Fourth, Christians Can <u>Know</u> That They Are Saved Because The Bible Says so.

"These things have I written unto you that believe on the name of the Son of God; that ye may **know** that ye **have** eternal life, and that ye may believe on the name of the Son of God." I John 5:13.

Do you have a Bible reason that you are going to Heaven? You can. This little book of the Bible was given to us to help us **know** that we know Him.

There is only one thing that can give us peace and assurance that we are going to Heaven when we die, and that is the Bible, God's Word. Can you say that you have a Bible reason that you are going to Heaven? Have you done what the Bible says to do to go to Heaven? Have you heard and believed the Gospel? If the answer is yes, check the box.

☐ I know, according to the Bible, that I am going to Heaven.

If you have checked all four boxes, God bless you. Quit doubting and start believing. Don't doubt what you believe and believe what you doubt. Believe God. Believe God's Word. Say, "Today, I believe God and my doubts have been removed." However, if you cannot say that you are a child of God, remove doubts today.

Remove Doubt

The Bible says, "For God so loved the world, that He gave His only begotten Son, that whosoever believeth in Him should not perish, but have everlasting life" John 3:16. This great Bible verse reveals four truths from the heart of God for all people.

Know That You Are Loved.

God wants you to know that **you are loved**. The Lord Jesus said, "For God so loved the world...." You are a part of this world, and God loves you. He gave His Son for you, and He wants you "...to know the love of Christ..." Ephesians 3:19.

Know That You Of Worth.

The Lord also wants you to know that **you are of worth**. We are so dear to God "...that He gave His only begotten Son...." The Bible teaches us that we are all sinners. "For all have sinned, and come short of the glory of God" Romans 3:23. And sin must be paid for. "For the wages of sin is death..." Romans 6:23.

But the Bible also teaches us that "...Christ died for our sins according to the scriptures" I Corinthians 15:3. God demonstrated His love for us and our worth to Him when He sent His Son to die in our place. The good news is that the Lord Jesus paid our sin debt in full when He died on the cross. "For He hath made Him to be sin for us..." II Corinthians 5:21.

Christ loved us and gave Himself for us as payment for our sin. You may ask, "How can God forgive **my** sin?" He can because of what Jesus did. "...While we were yet sinners, Christ died for us" Romans 5:8.

Know That You Can Have Hope.

God wants you to know that **you can have hope**. He said "...that whosoever believeth in Him should not perish...."

Life is fragile, and people are perishing. But Christ came "...that they might have life, and that they might have it more abundantly" John 10:10.

In a world where so many have lost hope, God wants us to know that the "...Lord Jesus Christ...is our hope" I Timothy 1:1. He rose from the dead, and He said, "...Because I live, **ye** shall live also" John 14:19.

Know That Your Life Can Have Purpose.

God wants you to know that **your life can have purpose**. He desires that we "...should not perish but have everlasting life." "And this is the promise that He hath promised us, even eternal life" I John 2:25. You may ask, "How can I receive God's promise of eternal life?"

> **Acknowledge** that you are a sinner, "for all have sinned, and come short of the glory of God" Romans 3:23.

> **Believe** that the Lord Jesus died for you, for "Christ died for our sins according to the scriptures" I Corinthians 15:3.

> **Call** upon the Lord to save you, "for whosoever shall call upon the name of the Lord shall be saved" Romans 10:13.

If you would be willing to turn to Christ in repentance and faith, pray this simple prayer of salvation:

"LORD, I know that I am a sinner, and I believe You died and rose again for me. I trust You to forgive me. Come into my heart and save me, and deliver me from sin." In Jesus' name I pray, AMEN.

The Lord Jesus said, "...I give unto them eternal life; and they shall never perish..." John 10:28. Everlasting life is ours when we receive Christ as our personal Saviour.

Now That You are A Christian:

Share your new-found faith with your family and friends. Acts 16:31-33. Identify with Christ through believer's baptism and become part of a local, Bible-believing church. Acts 2:41-47.

Becoming A Witness

"Therefore, if any man be in Christ, he is a new creature: old things are passed away; behold, all things are become new." II Corinthians 5:17. Every Christian should be prepared to share their personal testimony with the unsaved. A Christian's life should have power and influence and should reflect a touch of God on their life.

Sharing Your Personal Testimony

"But ye shall receive power, after that the Holy Ghost is come upon you: and ye shall be witnesses unto me both in Jerusalem, and in all Judea, and in Samaria, and unto the uttermost part of the earth." Acts 1:8.

Your personal testimony should be divided into three sections.

First, give a testimony about your life <u>before</u> receiving Christ.

Always use terminology people can relate to without bragging on sin and the devil. We must be careful not to give the impression that they must be "really bad" before they can be saved. Use terminology to describe your life before Christ by saying, "Before I came to know the Lord, there was____."

Fill in the blank with words such as: emptiness, fear, no direction, loneliness, lack of peace, or no purpose. These are things all people can relate to in their life.

Second, tell how you became a Christian.

We must <u>always include the Bible</u>. "So then faith cometh by hearing, and hearing by the Word of God" Romans 10:17. This is where we remove the three main reasons, or defenses, people use for not talking about their relationship with Christ.

1. Some say it's too personal to discuss.

2. Some say that no one can know for sure.

3. Some try to be smart alecks to scare you from talking to them.

You may wish to say, "I'm glad that I did not think talking about where I was going to spend eternity was too personal to talk about, and I'm so thankful I met someone who knew where they were going when they died." Remind people that you did what the Bible said to do to have peace and forgiveness, and it worked! God changed your life.

Third, tell what it means to be a Christian.

We should conclude our testimony by saying something like, "Since that day my life has never been the same. I have peace and purpose for living. It all began when someone cared enough about me to ask me a question. We must finish our testimony by asking the 100% QUESTION: **"If you died today are you 100% sure you would go to Heaven, or do you have some doubts?"**

"Seeking the praise of men will spoil your Christian work.

You cannot stand on a pedestal and hand out the Gospel."

JPM

The Power of A Personal Testimony

"But ye shall receive power, after that the Holy Ghost is come upon you: and ye shall be witnesses unto me both in Jerusalem, and in all Judea, and in Samaria, and unto the uttermost part of the earth." Acts 1:8.

Your testimony has the power to accomplish five things:

1. **Your testimony should create a desire in the hearts of others to want to know Christ.** The Bible says, "Blessed are they which do hunger and thirst after righteousness..." Matthew 5:6. In John 4:15, the woman at the well said to Jesus, "Sir, give me this water." Jesus created a desire in her heart to want to know God.

2. **Your testimony should take away objections people have for not listening.** Remember, "...the god of this world hath blinded the minds of them which believe not, lest the light of the glorious gospel of Christ, who is the image of God, should shine unto them" II Corinthians 4:4. The joy of our testimony should remove any objections people have for not listening.

3. **Your testimony should cause people to examine their lives.** The Bible says, "But let a man examine himself..." I Corinthians 11:28. It is human nature for people to relate what they hear and see to themselves. As you talk about your salvation experience, they will think about their own relationship with Christ or lack thereof.

4. **Your testimony should manifest the presence of Christ.** When we share our testimony, the unsaved can sense and feel God's presence. The Bible says, "...For this purpose the Son of God was manifested, that He might destroy the works of the devil" I John 3:8. Remember, God inhabits the praise of His people Psalm 22:3. It is in Christ's presence that people are saved.

5. **Your testimony should prepare the heart to receive the Word of God.** Your testimony is your light on God's work. The Bible says, "Let your **light** so shine before men, that they may see your good **work**s, and glorify your Father which is in heaven" Matthew 5:16.

Light: "Thy Word is a lamp unto my feet, and a light unto my path" Psalm 119:105. God's Word is His light, and <u>our word is our light</u>. When the Lord said, "Let your light…," He was talking about your words.

Work: "Being confident of this very thing, that He which hath begun a good work in you will perform it until the day of Jesus Christ" Philippians 1:6. The "work" in this verse is the change God has brought about in our lives. The "good work" in our lives is what the Lord has done for us.

These two things are like nutcrackers. On one side we have light, and on the other side, work. When we bring them together, they crack the hard heart so that we might plant the seed of God's Word. "Being born again, not of corruptible seed, but of incorruptible, by the word of God, which liveth and abideth for ever" I Peter 1:23. God's Word<u>must</u> get into their heart.

Having someone share their personal testimony in a meeting helps prepare others to receive Christ. It is always good to have a personal testimony planned for a Gospel meeting.

"Don't look for the faults
in others as you go through life,

And even when you find them,
it is wise and kind,
to be somewhat blind and look for the
virtues in them."

JPM

Getting A Grip On The Bible

"And take the helmet of salvation, and the sword of the Spirit, which is the word of God:" Ephesians 6:17.

Every Child of God should work at getting a working knowledge of the Bible. God says, "And these words, which I command thee this day, shall be in thine heart: And thou shalt teach them diligently unto thy children, and shalt talk of them when thou sittest in thine house, and when thou walkest by the way, and when thou liest down, and when thou risest up." Deuteronomy 6:6-7.

The Bible says, "...The people that do know their God shall be strong and do exploits." Daniel 11:32. Compare this verse with what Hosea says, "My people are destroyed for lack of knowledge..." Hosea 4:6. If we know God and His Word, we will be victorious. If we do not know God's Word, we will be defeated. We need to know the Bible.

We need the Bible for assurance of our salvation.

Paul said to Timothy, "And that from a child thou hast known the holy scriptures, which are able to make thee wise unto salvation through faith which is in Christ Jesus." II Timothy 3:15. In other words, Timothy grew up learning God's Word and having assurance of his salvation.

We need the Bible to keep our heart and life clean.

The Bible says, "Wherewithal shall a young man cleanse his way? by taking heed thereto according to Thy word." Psalm 119:9. As we spend time in the Bible, God's Word will search out our hearts. We learn from the Bible, "If we confess our sins, he is faithful and just to forgive us *our* sins, and to cleanse us from all unrighteousness." I John1:9.

We need the Bible to have direction for our life.

The Psalmist said, "Thy word is a lamp unto my feet, and a light unto my path." Psalm 119:105. God has a path for every life.

God's Word will show us the path. Job said about God and His Word, "...He marketh all my paths." Job 33:11. God wants every child of His to stay on track with His plan for their life.

We need the Bible to make right decisions in our life.

The Psalmist said, "...I will consider Thy testimonies." Psalm 119:95. In other words, we should consider God's Word before making life changing decisions. The quality of our life will be determined by the quality of our decisions. These are just a few reasons why we need to know God's Word. What we do with the Bible will determine what the Lord does with us.

How Can We Get a Grip on the Bible?

"Study to shew thyself approved unto God, a workman that needeth not to be ashamed, rightly dividing the word of truth." II Timothy 2:15. There are five methods by which we can get a firm grip on God's Word.

Hear it

"Faith cometh by hearing, and hearing by the Word of God." Romans 10:17. We hear the Word of God as it is preached and taught. There is a blessing for hearing the Word. "Blessed is he that readeth, and they that <u>hear</u> the words of this prophecy, and keep those things which are written therein: for the time is at hand." Revelation 1:3.

We forget 90% of what we hear. We encourage every Christian to take notes when the Bible is being taught. We will retain more of what we write down than what we only hear.

Read it

"Blessed is he that readeth..." Revelation 1:3. "Till I come, give attendance to reading..." I Timothy 4:13. We should have a schedule to read the Word of God. As we read, God speaks to our heart. We should mark verses that speak to us or verses that help us. We remember more of what we read than what we hear.

Study it

"Study to shew thyself approved unto God, a workman that needeth not to be ashamed, rightly dividing the word of truth." II Timothy 2:15. When we study the Bible, we are searching thru God's Word. "These were more noble than those in Thessalonica, in that they received the word with all readiness of mind, and searched the scriptures daily, whether those things were so." Acts 17:11.

We can study people, events, subjects, promises, doctrines, and the list could go on. The more methods we use to study the Bible the more we glean and retain from it.

Memorizing it

"Thy word have I hid in mine heart, that I might not sin against Thee." Psalm 119:11. As we put the Word of God to memory, we are hiding it in our hearts. Make a list of verses you want to put to memory.

Meditate on it

"This book of the law shall not depart out of thy mouth; but thou shalt meditate therein day and night, that thou mayest observe to do according to all that is written therein: for then thou shalt make thy way prosperous, and then thou shalt have good success." Joshua 1:8.

This is the most powerful method of getting a grip on God's Word. God promises success to those who meditate on His Word. (Psalm 1:1-6) It is while we meditate on the Word that the Holy Spirit teaches us the truths in God's Word.

"But the anointing which ye have received of Him abideth in you, and ye need not that any man teach you: but as the same anointing teacheth you of all things, and is truth, and is no lie, and even as it hath taught you, ye shall abide in Him." I John 2:27. This is the most powerful of all methods. This is when God opens our hearts and minds of understanding.

The Lord can bring to remembrance what we hide in our hearts. The Bible says, "But the Comforter, which is the Holy Ghost, whom the Father will send in My name, He shall teach you all things, and bring all things to your remembrance, whatsoever I have said unto you." John 14:26. God said when His people could not remember, "...He remembered for them..." Psalm 106:45.

When we pray for people who have hidden the Word of God in their hearts, the Holy Spirit can awaken the verse that "...liveth and abideth for ever..." I Peter 1:23. The verse that "...is a discerner of the thoughts and intents of the heart." Hebrews 4:12.

Getting A Grip On The Bible

(Illustrated with our hand)

1. The little finger represents hearing God's Word. If all we do is hear the Word, we will not be able to hold the Word.

2. The ring finger represents reading God's Word. We can hold the Word better with two fingers but still not much of a grip.

3. The middle finger represents studying God's Word. We get a better grip when we include this method, but it does not take much to pull it out of our hands.

4. The index finger (the trigger finger) represents memorizing the Word of God. This method gives us more of a grip, but we cannot hold on to it.

5. The thumb represents meditating on God's Word. This method strengthens all the others, and we have a good grip on God's Word when we use them all.

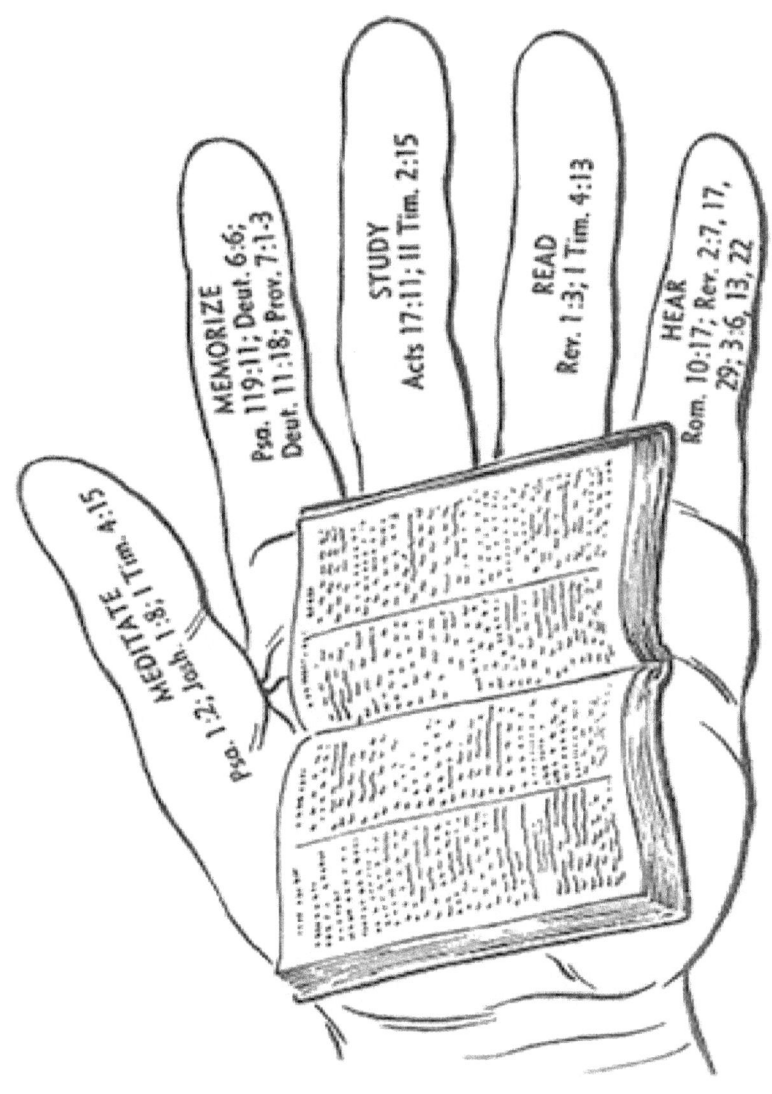

When teaching this lesson, have someone try to hold their Bible by only using three or four fingers but not using their thumb. Then pull it out of their hand. Next, let them use their thumb (meditate), which strengthens their grip. Then try to pull it out of their hand. This illustration shows how meditation strengthens all the others.

Becoming A Five Star Christian

"And they continued stedfastly in the apostles' doctrine and fellowship, and in breaking of bread, and in prayers." Acts 2:42-47, v. 42.

We all know what the five-star rating means. It means excellence; the best. Our desire for our children is to have God's best for their life. We want them to know God and to be people of faith. We want them to be practicing Christians. Five Star Christians are practicing Christians.

The five stars that make up the Five Star Christian Life are the foundations of the Christian life. They produce the roots that allow believers to be planted in the faith. Each star produces a certain fruit, and to have the fruit we must have the root.

Dr. Roberson said that, "Every victory in the believer's life is the result of doing these five things and every problem in the believer's life can be traced back to the neglect of these five things." If we want our children to grow in the LORD, to have victory, purpose of life, direction, peace, power over sin, faith, answered prayers, treasures in Heaven (the list could go on); they must become Five Star Christians. What are the five stars that make up the Five Star Christian?

★ The First Star Is Bible Reading

"And they continued stedfastly in the apostles' <u>doctrine</u>..." v. 42. "Blessed is he that readeth, and they that hear the words of this prophecy..." Revelation 1:3. Children need to know the importance of God's Word. We need to help them get a grip on God's Word: to read it, incorporate it into their daily life, and know its message. Bible reading produces:

- Faith "So then faith cometh by hearing, and hearing by the word of God." Romans 10:17.

- Direction for Life "Thy word is a lamp unto my feet, and a light unto my path." Psalm 119:105.

- Deliverance from Personal Battles "He sent his word, and healed them, and delivered them from their destructions." Psalm 107:20. If they incorporate the Bible into their daily life, they have added this star to their Christian life.

★ The Second Star Is Prayer

"And they continued...in <u>prayers</u>." v. 42. "Pray without ceasing." I Thessalonians 5:17,

Children need to know that their prayers make a difference. The little maid made a difference in Naaman's life. The Hebrew children made a difference through their prayers. Children should be encouraged to keep a prayer list and to talk about how the LORD has answered their prayers. Prayer produces:

The Blessing of God on our lives "Ye lust, and have not: ye kill, and desire to have, and cannot obtain: ye fight and war, yet ye have not, because ye ask not." James 4:2.

A Closeness to the LORD "Draw nigh to God, and he will draw nigh to you. Cleanse your hands, ye sinners; and purify your hearts, ye double minded." James 4:8.

Rewards in Heaven "And when he had taken the book, the four beasts and four and twenty elders fell down before the Lamb, having every one of them harps, and golden vials full of odours, which are the prayers of saints." Revelation 5:8. If our children have a prayer life, they have added this star to their Christian life.

★ The Third Star Is Faithfulness To Church

"And they continued stedfastly in...<u>fellowship</u>..." v. 42. "Not forsaking the assembling of ourselves together, as the manner of some is; but exhorting one another: and so much the more, as ye see the day approaching." Hebrews 10:25.

Children need to be connected to God's family. They should get to know members of the church and be familiar with them.

They need to know that church is not just a place to attend, but a place to serve the LORD. Children want something to do and there are many responsibilities they can have. There are jobs for children, such as:

1. Picking up trash
2. Straightening up books
3. Checking the bathrooms, etc.

Faithfulness to church will produce:

Encouragement in their life "Not forsaking the assembling of ourselves together, as the manner of some is; but exhorting one another: and so much the more, as ye see the day approaching...But exhort one another daily, while it is called To day; lest any of you be hardened through the deceitfulness of sin." Hebrews 10:25,3:13.

Fellowship with Like-Minded people "And they continued stedfastly in the apostles' doctrine and fellowship, and in breaking of bread, and in prayers." Acts 2:42.

"But if we walk in the light, as he is in the light, we have fellowship one with another, and the blood of Jesus Christ his Son cleanseth us from all sin." 1 John 1:7.

The Joy of the LORD in their life "I was glad when they said unto me, Let us go into the house of the LORD." Psalm 122:1. "...The joy of the LORD is your strength." Nehemiah 8:10. If they are faithful to church, they have added this star to their Christian life.

★ The Fourth Star Is Giving

"And sold their possessions and goods, and parted them to all men, as every man had need." Acts 2:45. "Give, and it shall be given unto you; good measure, pressed down, and shaken together, and running over, shall men give into your bosom. For with the same measure that ye mete withal it shall be measured to you again." Luke 6:38. Children need to be taught how to be good stewards of their time, talent, and treasure.

They should give a portion of their day to the LORD. Children have a special gift (talent), and they should be encouraged to use it for the LORD. Our children need to be taught how to honor God with their treasure (money). Teaching children early about the importance of giving will help protect them against "...the love of money which is the root of all evil."

Being a good steward produces:

The Windows of Heaven Open in our lives "Bring ye all the tithes into the storehouse, that there may be meat in mine house, and prove me now herewith, saith the LORD of hosts, if I will not open you the windows of heaven, and pour you out a blessing, that there shall not be room enough to receive it." Malachi 3:10.

Being Blessed by others "Give, and it shall be given unto you; good measure, pressed down, and shaken together, and running over, shall men give into your bosom. For with the same measure that ye mete withal it shall be measured to you again." Luke 6:38.

Treasures in Heaven "But lay up for yourselves treasures in heaven, where neither moth nor rust doth corrupt, and where thieves do not break through nor steal: For where your treasure is, there will your heart be also." Matthew 6:20-21. If children are good stewards of their gifts, they have added this star to their Christian life.

★ The Fifth Star Is Witnessing

"And they, continuing daily with one accord in the temple, and breaking bread from house to house, did eat their meat with gladness and singleness of heart" Acts 2:46. "But ye shall receive power, after that the Holy Ghost is come upon you: and ye shall be witnesses unto me both in Jerusalem, and in all Judaea, and in Samaria, and unto the uttermost part of the earth." Acts 1:8.

Children want to share their faith. There is such a bold innocence about a child's witness. Children will speak to anyone — loved ones, family members, friends, neighbors, teachers, classmates — the list could go on! Many have been brought to Christ through the witness of a child. We help children share their faith and give them a "Gospel Award" when they learn the Gospel and become a witness. Being a faithful witness produces:

- **Rewards at the Judgment Seat of Christ** "For what is our hope, or joy, or crown of rejoicing? Are not even ye in the presence of our Lord Jesus Christ at his coming? For ye are our glory and joy." I Thessalonians 2:19-20.

- **Compassion in a Believer's life** "...When he saw the multitudes, he was moved with compassion..." Matthew 9:35-36.

- **Eternal Joy over a life given to the LORD** "The fruit of the righteous is a tree of life; and he that winneth souls is wise." Proverbs 11:30. "And they that be wise shall shine as the brightness of the firmament; and they that turn many to righteousness as the stars for ever and ever." Daniel 12:3.

If they have become a faithful witness, they have added this star to their Christian life. Helping our children become Five Star Christians helps them have the strongest foundation they can have.

"There is no book that tells about this Gospel but the Bible.

Therefore, the great object in all our work has been to get this Book into the hands and hearts of all."

JPM

A Self-Test To Becoming a 5.0 Christian

"...examine yourselves" II Corinthians *13:5*

To be a 5.0 Christian (a Five Star Christian) means we are following the example given to us by the first century believers. They turned the world upside down with the Gospel and won their families, friends, cities, and the world by doing five things faithfully. The five things they did are recorded in the Bible in Acts 2:42-47. Doing these five things will make <u>you</u> a Five Star Christian.

The following self-test will help you see how strong a Christian you have become. Here is how it works. Read each question and give yourself a score from 0 – 5. Use this key to determine your answer.

0. Never   1. Occasionally   2. Most of the time

3. Almost always   4. Rarely miss   5. Never miss

Once you have finished each question add the total and then divide that number by 20. You will get a number like 3.75, 1.25 or 4.50 which represents your star rating. Each month you can retest yourself and determine if you are growing as a Christian.

__1. I read the Bible every day.

__2. I am studying the Bible.

__3. I meditate and memorize God's Word.

__4. I am teaching the Bible to others.

__5. I pray daily.

__6. I have an up-to-date prayer list.

__7. I have prayer promises that I claim.

__8. I pray with others and for others.

__9. I am faithful to all three services (except for sickness or work).

__10. I attend Sunday school.

__11. I have a place of service in my church.

__12. I am a leader in my home church.

__13. I tithe faithfully.

__14. I give above my tithe.

__15. I give to missions regularly.

__16. I ask the Lord to give through me.

__17. I am a faithful witness.

__18. I carry tracts at all times.

__19. I have shared my faith with my family members and friends.

__20. I faithfully attend our soul winning outreach.

0. Never **1.** Occasionally **2.** Most of the time **3.** Almost always **4.** Rarely miss **5.** Never miss

> *"I have never known a Christian to backslide who continued the daily, prayerful study of the Bible."*
> JPM

Sharing The Gospel
(God Loves You Tract)

"For God so loved the world, that He gave His only begotten Son, that whosoever believeth in Him should not perish, but have everlasting life" John 3:16.

This great Bible verse reveals four truths from the heart of God for all people.

We Are Loved.

God wants us to know that **we are loved**. The Lord Jesus said, "For God so loved the world…." You are a part of this world, and God loves you. He gave His Son for you, and He wants you "…to know the love of Christ…" Ephesians 3:19.

We Are Of Worth.

The Lord also wants us to know that **we are of worth**. We are so dear to God "…that He gave His only begotten Son…." The Bible teaches us that we are all sinners. "For all have sinned, and come short of the glory of God" Romans 3:23. And sin must be paid for. "For the wages of sin is death…" Romans 6:23.

But the Bible also teaches us that "…Christ died for our sins according to the scriptures" I Corinthians 15:3. God demonstrated His love for us and our worth to Him when He sent His Son to die in our place. The good news is that the Lord Jesus paid our sin debt in full when He died on the cross. "For He hath made Him to be sin for us…" II Corinthians 5:21.

Christ loved us and gave Himself for us as payment for our sin. You may ask, "How can God forgive **my** sin?" He can because of what Jesus did. "…While we were yet sinners, Christ died for us" Romans 5:8.

We Can Have Hope.

God wants us to know that **we can have hope**. He said "…that whosoever believeth in Him should not perish…."

Life is fragile, and people are perishing. But Christ came "...that they might have life, and that they might have it more abundantly" John 10:10. In a world where so many have lost hope, God wants us to know that the "...Lord Jesus Christ...is our hope" I Timothy 1:1. He rose from the dead, and He said, "...Because I live, ye shall live also" John 14:19.

We Can Have Purpose.

God wants us to know that **we can have purpose** in life. He desires that we "...should not perish but have everlasting life." "And this is the promise that He hath promised us, even eternal life" I John 2:25. You may ask, "How can I receive God's promise of eternal life?"

> **Acknowledge** that you are a sinner, "for all have sinned, and come short of the glory of God" Romans 3:23.
>
> **Believe** that the Lord Jesus died for you, for "Christ died for our sins according to the scriptures" I Corinthians 15:3.
>
> **Call** upon the Lord to save you, "for whosoever shall call upon the name of the Lord shall be saved" Romans 10:13.

If you would be willing to turn to Christ in repentance and faith, pray this simple prayer of salvation:

"LORD, I know that I am a sinner, and I believe You died and rose again for me. I trust You to forgive me. Come into my heart and save me. Help me to live for You. In Jesus' name, Amen."

The Lord Jesus said, "...I give unto them eternal life; and they shall never perish..." John 10:28. Everlasting life is ours when we receive Christ as our personal Saviour.

Now That You are A Christian:

Share your new-found faith with your family and friends. Acts 16:31-33. Identify with Christ through believer's baptism and become part of a local, Bible-believing church. Acts 2:41-47.

Using The Gospel Colors

The disciples learned from the LORD Jesus how to use God's creation to teach the great truths about God's love and His plan for life. The Gospel colors, from God's creation to teach the Gospel, was first used by famed English preacher Charles Haddon Spurgeon in a message on January 11, 1866.

Spurgeon was preaching to orphans who could not read. He used three colors of paper, black, red, and white, to teach the glorious Gospel of Christ. He used black to represent man's sin, red to represent Christ's shed blood and death, and white to represent God's forgiveness and our new life.

This method of presenting the Gospel caught on quickly. Hudson Taylor took it to the mission field. D.L. Moody added a fourth color, gold, to represent God's love and plan for man, and used it across America in his meeting.

A fifth color, green, was added to represent growing and going. Untold millions have been won to Christ over the years by using these colors to teach the Gospel.

We here at Five Star Christian Ministries have designed a beautiful **Gospel Pin** and **Gospel Bracelet** with the five colors to be used in sharing the Gospel of Christ worldwide.

"It is better to die and go to heaven than to live like a coward "

JPM

The Gospel Pin & Gospel Bracelet

GOLD – God Loves You and Has A Plan for Your Life

"For God so loved the world, that he gave his only begotten Son, that whosoever believeth in him should not perish, but have everlasting life." John 3:16. The Lord is., not willing that any should perish, but that all should come to repentance." II Peter 3:9.

BLACK – We Are All Sinners

"For all have sinned, and come short of the glory of God;" Romans 3:23.

"Wherefore, as by one man sin entered into the world, and death by sin; and so death passed upon all men, for that all have sinned:" Romans 5:12.

"For the wages of sin is death; but the gift of God is eternal life through Jesus Christ our Lord." Romans 6:23.

RED – Christ Died for Our Sins

"But God commendeth his love toward us, in that, while we were yet sinners, Christ died for us." Romans 5:8. "For he hath made him to be sin for us, who knew no sin; that we might be made the righteousness of God in him." II Corinthians 5:21. "...Ye were not redeemed with corruptible things ...But with the precious blood of Christ:" I Peter 1:18-19.

WHITE – Christ Rose From the Grave and Offers Forgiveness to All

"Christ died for our sins according to the scriptures; And that he was buried, and that he rose again the third day according to the scriptures:" I Corinthians 15:3^b-4.

"That if thou shalt confess with thy mouth the Lord Jesus, and shalt believe in thine heart that God hath raised him from the dead, thou shalt be saved...For whosoever shall call upon the name of the Lord shall be saved." Romans 10:9,13.

GREEN – New Life for the Believer. He is to Grow and Go Tell Others.

Jesus said, "...because I live, ye shall live also." John 14:19. "Therefore if any man be in Christ, he is a new creature: old things are passed away; behold, all things are become new." II Corinthians 5:17. "And he said unto them, Go ye into all the world, and preach the gospel to every creature." Mark 16:15.

Children

"And these words, which I command thee this day, shall be in thine heart: And thou shalt teach them diligently unto thy children." Deuteronomy 6:1-15, v. 6-7

Children, what a word! Our hearts are softened by the very mention of it. Fond memories fill our minds when we think of it. What would someone do who truly loves their children? How far would they go to protect them? How much would they give to prepare and train them?

We who are in the LORD's work have a great responsibility to make sure children are given the same Christian foundation that God has given to us. A look at today's leaders reveals our need to prepare this generation of children and young people.

"Train up a child in the way he should go: and when he is old, he will not depart from it." Proverbs 22:6. What do children need today? I have done an acrostic on the word CHILDREN to help us understand what children need.

Christ	Mark 10:14b-1
Honor	Romans 13:7
Influence	Romans 14:7
Love	Matthew 22:37
Direction	Proverbs 14:12
Rejoice	Philippians 4:4
Encouragement	Isaiah 41:6-7a
Narrow	Philippians 3:13

CHRIST

"Suffer the little children to come unto me, and forbid them not: for of such is the kingdom of God. Verily I say unto you, Whosoever shall not receive the kingdom of God as a little child, he shall not enter therein." Mark 10:13-16, v. 14b-15.

The LORD Jesus wants children to be saved. The most important decision in any child's life is the one they make about Christ. Make sure children understand the Gospel and know why Jesus died.

Children Are Ready To Receive Christ

"And that from a child thou hast known the holy scriptures, which are able to make thee wise unto salvation through faith which is in Christ Jesus." II Timothy 3:15. We think that children need an adult understanding about salvation, but the LORD Jesus said, "Whosoever shall not receive the kingdom of God **as a little child**, he shall not enter therein." We have it backwards. It is not that a child needs an adult faith; it is adults that need a childlike faith.

Children Bring Rewards In Heaven

"...For of such is the kingdom of God." v. 14.

The majority of those who come to Christ are children. It has been my experience to discover that over 50% of the believers that I speak to have come to Christ before their 16th birthday. Someone has said, "The only thing we can take to Heaven with us is people." Think of all the rewards waiting in Heaven because of children being reached.

HONOR

"Render therefore to all their dues: tribute to whom tribute is due; custom to whom custom; fear to whom fear; honor to whom honor." Romans 13:7. Children need to be taught how to honor. No one has ever succeeded in life who failed to honor. There is so much dishonor in our nation today.

Honor The Lord

"Honor the LORD with thy substance, and with the first fruits of all thine increase" Proverbs 3:9. Children need to know the importance of honoring the LORD. "The fear of the LORD is the instruction of wisdom; and before honour is humility." Proverbs 15:33. Children, who honor the LORD, stay right with God.

Honor Parents

"Children, obey your parents in the Lord: for this is right. Honour thy father and mother (which is the first commandment with promise,)" Ephesians 6:1-2. Children should obey their parents "for this is right," but more importantly, they should honor their parents. Children who do not learn to honor in the home will not honor outside the home.

Honor Leadership

"Honour all men. Love the brotherhood. Fear God. Honour the king." I Peter 2:17. God expects His people to honor leadership. We honor leadership in our church, in our community, and in our country. Children who have been taught to honor accomplish great things.

INFLUENCE

"For none of us liveth to himself, and no man dieth to himself." Romans 14:7. Children have influence. Children use their influence daily. A child can say, "I don't like to eat there!" and you will write that restaurant off. If a child says they did not like the Sunday School class or church service, their parents will more than likely not come back.

Their Influence Can Make A Difference In The Home

"Lo, children are an heritage of the LORD: and the fruit of the womb is his reward. As arrows are in the hand of a mighty man; so are children of the youth. Happy is the man that hath his quiver full of them: they shall not be ashamed, but they shall speak with the enemies in the gate." Psalm 127:3-5.

Children bring such joy into a home. Parents want to see their children grow and learn. They will listen to them quote Bible verses or sing the songs of the faith. Someone has said that when you take a child by the hand, you take a mother by the heart.

Their Influence Can Make A Difference In Their Home And School

"But thou art holy, O thou that inhabitest the praises of Israel." Psalm 22:3. Remember, the Bible teaches us that the LORD inhabits the praise of his people. When children go to school or other places, they can bring joy and praise to God. An excited child can accomplish more to fill up a Sunday School class or Sunday School bus than two dedicated adults.

LOVE

"Jesus said unto him, Thou shalt love the Lord thy God with all thy heart, and with all thy soul, and with all thy mind." Matthew 22:37. "God is love," and He created us in His image. Children are full of love. They will sometimes love what they should not love. All children need to be taught to guard their hearts.

Love The Good

"Hate the evil and love the good..." Amos 5:15. Children need to know the difference between good and evil. There are those who call evil good and good evil. Love is a positive force in a child's life. They will become what they love.

Love Not The World

"Love not the world, neither the things that are in the world. If any man love the world, the love of the Father is not in him. For all that is in the world, the lust of the flesh, and the lust of the eyes, and the pride of life, is not of the Father, but is of the world. And the world passeth away, and the lust thereof: but he that doeth the will of God abideth forever." I John 2:15-17.

There are three things about the world that we are not to love:
- "...the lust of the flesh..."   Pleasure
- "...the lust of the eyes..."   Possessions
- "...the pride of life..."   Pride

Remember that "...the <u>love</u> of money is <u>the root</u> of all evil..." I Timothy 6:10.

DIRECTION

"There is a way which seemeth right unto a man, but the end thereof are the ways of death." Proverbs 14:12. Children need direction for life. If we are not careful, they will "walk in the counsel of the ungodly" Psalm 1:1.

Direction Comes From God's Word

"Thy word is a lamp unto my feet, and a light unto my path." Psalm 119:105.

The Lord will give His children directions for life through His Word. Sometimes He will cause us "to know the way" Psalm 143:8. God has a path for every life. "...He maketh all my paths." Job 33:11.

Direction Comes From God's People

"Train up a child in the way he should go: and when he is old, he will not depart from it." Proverbs 22:6.

We have the responsibility to show the next generation the way. "Thus saith the LORD, Stand ye in the ways, and see, and ask for the old paths, where is the good way, and walk therein, and ye shall find rest for your souls. But they said, We will not walk therein." Jeremiah 6:16.

The old path is still the best path for young and old. Help children stay on track with God's plan for their life.

REJOICE

"Rejoice in the Lord alway: and again I say, Rejoice." Philippians 4:4.

Children need to keep a good spirit. They need to find the source of happiness and learn that you can have joy no matter what is happening around you.

The Joy Of The Lord Is Our Strength

"For the joy of the LORD is your strength." Nehemiah 8:10. A joyful Christian is a strong Christian. The disciples "did eat their meat with gladness and singleness of heart." Acts 2:46. They were joyful Christians.

The Joy Of The Lord Is How We Worship

"Serve the LORD with gladness: come before his presence with singing." Psalm 100:2. Children need to be taught early in life how to worship the LORD. Children love Jesus and they love to tell others about Him.

ENCOURAGEMENT

"They helped every one his neighbour; and every one said to his brother, Be of good courage. So the carpenter encouraged the goldsmith..." Isaiah 41:6-7. Children need to be encouraged in the LORD. They need to be encouraged to do God's will with their life. "The carpenter and the goldsmith" were encouraged. Not all children are going into the LORD's work, but all should be fulltime Christians.

We Are To Encourage One Another Daily

"But exhort one another daily, while it is called Today; lest any of you be hardened through the deceitfulness of sin." Hebrews 3:13. One of the daily duties of a Christian is to encourage someone daily. A pat on the back or "That a boy" or "That a girl" goes a long way in a child's life.

Children Will Encourage You

"And let us consider one another to provoke unto love and to good works: Not forsaking the assembling of ourselves together, as the manner of some is; but exhorting one another: and so much the more, as ye see the day approaching." Hebrews 10:24-25. I cannot count the number of cards, notes, and pictures that children have given me over the years. Sometimes these have been my only words of encouragement. They have considered me and provoked me "unto love and to good works."

NARROW

"Because strait is the gate, and narrow is the way, which leadeth unto life, and few there be that find it." Matthew 7:14. Staying on track is one of the most difficult things to do in the Christian life. How can children stay on track?

Looking Unto Jesus

"Wherefore seeing we also are compassed about with so great a cloud of witnesses, let us lay aside every weight, and the sin which doth so easily beset us, and let us run with patience the race that is set before us, Looking unto Jesus the author and finisher of our faith; who for the joy that was set before him endured the cross, despising the shame, and is set down at the right hand of the throne of God." Hebrews 12:1-2. Looking up keeps us on track. It does not take a lot of knowledge or faith to look. Keep your eyes on Jesus and stay on track with your life. God's path is narrow and one's path through life should be narrow, "...this one thing I do..."

Forget The Failures

"Brethren...this one thing I do, forgetting those things which are behind, and reaching forth unto those things which are before" Philippians 3:13.
Some children come from very difficult homes. They have witnessed failures. Many children have been in homes that failed. Mother or Father has left them. Sometimes children think their parents' failure is their fault.

The Gospel Award

(The Gospel Award Program Is Explained On Page 98)

The Gospel Award program is our follow-up program for children. It helps them get assurance of their salvation and get started in their newfound faith. The program is simple enough for a child to do and yet powerful in how it transforms the child, their home and their family.

My wife and I began teaching the children, who rode our bus to Sunday School many years ago, to memorize what we called the Romans Road, God's message of salvation.

The children, whose parents help their children work on their verses, become convinced of their own need of salvation. Over the years we have seen scores of families come to the Saviour using this simple program. It works!

How Does It Work

After children have trusted Christ as their personal Savior, they are encouraged to work on receiving the Gospel Award. The Gospel Award is a beautiful 8x10 certificate that has their name and their accomplishment on it.

We present them with their certificate in one of our morning services where parents are invited to attend. We make Gospel Award Sunday a big day in the young person's life. Parents receive a special letter from the pastor inviting them to this service and informing them of their child being honored.

In most cases a visit has been made to the home where parents are prayed with and encouraged to trust the Lord Jesus as their personal Saviour. (Later we will give some instructions on making the visit to the home)

The Gospel Award program works by giving the children three things to do.

1. Each week the children memorize one of the Gospel verses. We ask parents to help their children by listening to them say it and initialing the space by the verse.

2. Once the children have memorized all the verses, we ask the parent to make sure they can tell the story of Jesus by using their Gospel bracelet and the Bible verses that they have memorized.

3. Children are encouraged to share the Gospel, using the bracelet, with a family member and a friend.

The parents then sign the form stating that their child have completed all the requirements to receive their award. We then prepare the award and inform the family of the special service for their child.

You can only imagine how powerful the witness has been in that home with the children memorizing Bible verses, singing the songs we teach them, and keeping their prayer and devotion times.

The **Gospel Award Program** has been developed to reach children, and their parents with the Gospel. Jesus said,

"Suffer the little children to come unto me, and forbid them not: for of such is the kingdom of God." Mark 10:13.

Monsters Are Coming

By Tom Sexton

It's not the monsters across the sea,

That's coming for you and me.

It's not the crazy man,

Who now has a nuke in his hand.

It's the evil we have spun,

With our failure to do what needed done.

It's the Sunday School bus we had to park,

Leaving boys and girls sitting in the dark.

It's the children we failed to reach,

It's the Bible class we wouldn't teach.

It's all who failed to do their part,

That's given us monsters,

With no Jesus in their heart.

Security Of Believers

The Lord Jesus said, "My sheep hear My voice, and I know them, and they follow Me: And I give unto them eternal life; and they shall never perish, neither shall any man pluck them out of My hand. My Father, which gave them Me, is greater than all; and no man is able to pluck them out of My Father's hand." John 10:27-29.

Did Christ mean what He said, and did He say what He meant? Of course He did. The Lord Jesus always spoke Truth. So, how secure are we as believers? What if we do not feel like a Christian? What if we do not always act like a Christian? Do we still have eternal life?

For the answer to these and many other questions let us look at God's Word.

Salvation Is A Gift

Romans 6:23, "...the gift of God is eternal life through Jesus Christ our Lord."
There are two words that every Christian should know: relationship and fellowship. We are brought into the family of God when we receive Jesus Christ by faith. This relationship is eternal. Our mistakes and failures affect our fellowship but not our relationship. Carefully read the following:

"If we say that we have no sin, we deceive ourselves, and the truth is not in us. If we confess our sins, He is faithful and just to forgive us our sins, and to cleanse us from all unrighteousness:" I John 1:8-9.

"And whatsoever we ask, we receive of Him, because we keep His commandments, and do those things that are pleasing in His sight." I John 3:22.

Our going to heaven, when we die, is the result of our relationship with Christ. For God to bless us here and for us to be used of the Lord, in this life, it is determined by our fellowship with Christ. We can break fellowship with the Lord, but we will never lose our relationship with Christ.

Nothing Can Separate Us From God

"Who shall separate us from the love of Christ? shall tribulation, or distress, or persecution, or famine, or nakedness, or peril, or sword? Nay, in all these things we are more than conquerors through Him that loved us. For I am persuaded, that neither death, nor life, nor angels, nor principalities, nor powers, nor things present, nor things to come, Nor height, nor depth, nor any other creature, shall be able to separate us from the love of God, which is in Christ Jesus our Lord." Romans 8:35-39.

It is impossible for anything to separate us from God and His Word says, "...Neither shall any man pluck them out of My hand." John 10:28. If no man can pluck us out of God's hands, then we cannot pluck ourselves out of God's hands either.

The Christian is sealed by the Holy Spirit "ye were sealed with that Holy Spirit of promise." Ephesians 1:13. "For ye have not received the spirit of bondage again to fear; but ye have received the Spirit of adoption, whereby we cry, Abba, Father. The Spirit itself beareth witness with our spirit, that we are the children of God:" Romans 8:15-16. Being sealed by the Holy Spirit gives us the assurance that we belong to Christ and that He will return for us.

The Bible Says That There Is No Condemnation

"There is therefore now no condemnation to them which are in Christ Jesus, who walk not after the flesh, but after the Spirit." Romans 8:1. The child of God will never stand in the same judgment with the unsaved. We will one day give an account of our lives as to what we have done with our life, but we will never be judged and cast into Hell.

Jesus promised to preserve our relationship forever. He said, "All that the Father giveth Me shall come to Me; and him that cometh to Me I will in no wise cast out." John 6:37.

Forever With Jesus

Knowing You Lord

Makes my life worth living

With all its twists and all its turns

The time we've share together

Is what my heart forever yearns

Everyone lives somewhere forever

One day we'll see it's true

My forever would be so lonely

If Your love I never knew

Your love for me has never faltered

No matter what I have gone through

And when this journey is over

I choose my forever to be lived with You

Yes, everyone lives somewhere forever

Your love for me will never die, 'tis true

That's why I'm choosing my forever

To be lived in Heaven with you

The Power of Gospel Tracts

"I am not ashamed of the gospel of Christ: for it is the power of God unto salvation to every one that believeth; to the Jew first, and also to the Greek." Romans 1:16.

Handing out Gospel tracts is something every Christian can do. One does not have to be a seasoned saint to tell others what Jesus is doing in their life and give them a Gospel tract.

1. Believers who give out Gospel tracts win personal victories.
Every victory in the Christian life is won in the presence of the Lord. The Bible says, "If we walk in the light, as he is in the light, we have fellowship one with another, and the blood of Jesus Christ his Son cleanseth us from all sin." I John 1:7. It is hard to have a bad habit in the presence of Jesus. People who hand out Gospel tracts are walking with Jesus and winning personal victories. Sharing our faith is the first step in winning victory.

2. Believers who give out Gospel tracts discover God's will.
If we want to know God's will for our life, we must first be willing to do God's will with our life. Start telling people how to know the Lord Jesus as their personal Saviour and the Lord will let you "see your calling" I Corinthians 1:26. He will show you where you fit in His plan for the ages. Believers who give Gospel tracts discover God's will for their life.

3. Believers giving out Gospel tracts are protected by the Lord.
Jesus promised His presence as we go. He said, "lo I am with you alway." Matthew 28:20.

The good news is that all believers, who share their faith, are protected by the presence of Christ. I have learned the devil's crowd avoids people who are talking about Jesus and walking with Him. Christians who hand out Gospel tracts discover their witnessing repels the devil's crowd and attracts hungry hearted people.

4. God begins a work in the one who receives a Gospel tract.

The Bible says, "Being confident of this very thing, that he which hath begun a good work in you will perform it until the day of Jesus Christ:" Philippians 1:6. Every time we give someone a Gospel tract, a work of God begins in their life.

The Lord Jesus said, "If I be lifted up from the earth, will draw all men unto me." John 12:32. How many people do you want to start a work of God in their life? Give them a Gospel tract and it begins.

5. Every Gospel tract we give someone is recorded in eternity.

According to the Bible, God keeps up with all we do in getting the Gospel to people. We read where the psalmist said "...my wanderings...are...in thy book." Psalms 56:8. This verse teaches us that God has a book about our life and work, and He records everything we do for our future meeting with Him.

One day we will be rewarded for what we do for God in this life. The Bible says, "For we must all appear before the judgment seat of Christ; that every one may receive the things done in his body, according to that he hath done, whether it be good or bad." II Corinthians 5:10.

In other words, every deed we do in getting the Word of God to people and sharing our faith will one day be made known to all. What people do with the Gospel tract we give them will determine where they spend eternity. If they say "Yes" to Jesus and His gift of eternal life, they will be in Heaven.

If they say "No" to the Gospel, they will be separated from God forever. The day they received a Gospel tract will be remembered by them forever and is recorded in their forever. Everyone will live somewhere forever and one day we will see it is true.

The Gospel Challenge

Jesus said, "For I came down from heaven, not to do mine own will, but the will of him that sent me." John 6:38. From the time of the baptism of Jesus until His ascension, He spent approximately 1200 days in His public ministry. Jesus was on a mission from God when he came into this world, and now His mission, is our mission.

He began His public ministry by preaching the Gospel and He ended His public ministry by commissioning His followers, us, to carry on the great work He began. Take the challenge and give out Gospel tracts every day. Here are tips for giving out Gospel tracts.

1. Set a personal goal each day of how many tracts you will give out, and say, "This one thing I do." Philippians 3:13.

2. Carry Gospel tracts on your person at all times, and say, "I am ready." Romans 1:15.

3. Pray for the people who receive a Gospel tract from you. Pray "the Word of the Lord may have free course and be glorified." II Thessalonians 3:1.

The Gospel Pledge

I pledge allegiance to the glorious Gospel of Christ.

God's message for all people.

I will faithfully publish it among all nations until the Lord returns.

For I am not ashamed of the Gospel of Christ,

For it is the power of God unto salvation

To everyone that believeth

To the Jew first, and also to the Greek.

Name_____

Date_____

By Signing I accept The Gospel Challenge

Having A Gospel Hour

"And there they preached the gospel." Acts 14:7

Having a Gospel Hour ministry allows our churches to fulfill the mission Christ gave us in Acts 1:8.

We can have a Gospel meeting anywhere people will gather. I can remember many men and women, who were faithful members of the Highland Park Baptist Church back in the day, reporting on services they had at the places of businesses they worked, such as factories, mills, offices, lunchrooms etc. The men who were conducting these meetings would tell of coworkers coming to Christ in those meetings.

I was recently reminded of one of the pioneers in church planting in south Florida named Spencer (Spink) Williams. He started a Gospel meeting during lunch time at a Hosiery mill where he worked. Scores of co-workers were saved and nine men who worked at the mill were called into the ministry out of his Hosiery mill meetings. What he and many others of his generation started, is what I am calling "Gospel Hours."

Gospel Hours can be started in any place where we find people. Gospel meetings can be held in day-cares, nursing homes, assisted living centers, schools from kindergarten through college, factories, hospitals, parks and recreation areas, resorts, and a host of other places.

The door is wide open. People are waiting for us to come to them with the Gospel. We must find a way to reach our cities for Christ. Every adult Sunday School class including teens, can be involved in the Gospel Hour ministry, because of the great need for workers in this powerful ministry.

I was driving down Highway 25 in Johnson County South Carolina back in the late 80s when I noticed a migrant camp with many of the workers sitting around. The camp was an old farmhouse with some new facilities in the back to house the workers.

In the front yard of the farmhouse was a camper, which I later discovered was where the crew chief stayed.

I knocked on the camper door and ask if I could have a Gospel meeting with the workers. He wanted me to explain a little bit about what I meant. He agreed to let me have a meeting. Then he asked, "When would you like to have the meeting?" I told him now because it was in the afternoon, and everybody was finished working.

I gathered the people around the front porch and sang a little chorus, "God Loves You & I Love You" to a tune I had learned from their Island. I shared a brief message on John 3:16. The Spirit of God came down in that meeting and many of those precious people trusted Christ as their personal Saviour.

I stayed about 40 minutes after the service, and we were all weeping and rejoicing over what God had done. Over fifty had been saved. I discovered there was a hand full of believers who were migrant workers in that camp, and they had been praying God would work in their camp. Then I knew why the Lord led me there.

God opened my mind and heart of understanding, and I realized this is something our church could do. I told the church on Wednesday night about this glorious meeting. After the service, a lady came up to me and told me she was a nurse who worked for the health department in Johnson County and had a map with all the migrant camps on it. She asked if I would like to have a copy of the map. I said yes!

I took the map and found other camps where we could have Gospel meetings. Some of the men in the church went with me and helped conduct more meetings. Area pastors heard about what was happening and joined us.

These workers were only in our area for a short while. We conducted forty meetings and saw over eleven hundred souls saved. I received many letters from these precious people when they returned home rejoicing that they had trusted Christ in our nation.

When my wife and I moved to south Florida to start the Gulf Coast Baptist Church, one of the faithful preachers who had been helping me in this new ministry Brother Melvin Minitour, took over the ministry I had started with the migrant workers, and has seen thousands come to Christ.

The Bible says about the first century Christians, "And they...preached the gospel in many villages of the Samaritans." Acts 8:25.

Let me say again, Gospel Hours can be started in any place where we find people. We want to add more. To God be the glory, at the writing of this our church has 125 Gospel Hours every month and by years end we want to increase that number.

Questions to consider.
1. Do you want to reach the unreached with the Gospel in your city?
2. Is there an example of first century Christians starting Gospel Hours?
3. Where can we start Gospel Hours?
4. Who can have part in the Gospel Hour ministry?
5. What days of the week can we have Gospel Hour services?
6. Does someone need to be called to preach to start a Gospel Hour?
7. Is there material we can use in this new ministry?
8. How do we get started?

How Do We Start A Gospel Hour?

"And Jesus went about all the cities and villages, teaching in their synagogues, and preaching the gospel of the kingdom, and healing every sickness and every disease...But when he saw the multitudes, he was moved with compassion on them, because they fainted, and were scattered abroad, as sheep having no shepherd.

Then saith he unto his disciples, The harvest truly *is* plenteous, but the labourers *are* few; Pray ye therefore the Lord of the harvest, that he will send forth labourers into his harvest." Matthew 9:35-28

How do we start a Gospel Hour? We have answered the questions: What is a Gospel Hour? Why do we have Gospel Hours? Where should we start Gospel Hours? Now we come to: How do we start a Gospel Hour?

These five steps are how we start all new ministries including Gospel Hours.

See the need.

Jesus said, "behold, I say unto you, Lift up your eyes, and <u>look</u> on the fields; for they are white already to harvest." John 4:35.

Learn about the demographics of your area. How many different people groups in your county? How many students in your schools? Let the Lord open your eyes to see the need.

Enlist and train workers.

Jesus said, "The harvest truly *is* plenteous, but the labourers *are* few; Pray ye therefore the Lord of the harvest, that he will send forth labourers into his harvest." Mathew 9:37-38.

Once you see the need talk about it to the Lord and other believers. God will give you someone to help carry the burden. Take the time to train new workers. Use this material.

Provide needed material.

Jesus said, "And the gospel must first be published among all nations." Mark 13:10. You may need to print or purchase material in the languages you are trying to reach.

Find a location.

The Bible says when Paul started the church in Philippi that "they went out of the prison, and entered into *the house of* Lydia: and when they had seen the brethren, they comforted them, and departed." Acts 16:40.

Lydia opened her heart to the Lord, she opened her house to the Church, and she opened her purse to missions.

Set a date and start.

Everything that gets going for God has a starting time. The Bible says about the wild man, who got saved in the Lords earthly ministry, and how he got started, "And he departed, and began to publish in Decapolis how great things Jesus had done for him: and all *men* did marvel." Mark 5:20.

We read, "And he…began." Amen! If I were an artist, I would paint a picture of him heading home rejoicing, walking away from the disciples cheering him on. I would paint the Lord Jesus smiling, looking up into Heaven.

Being On Team Jesus
Working With God and Doing Our Part

"We are labourers together with God." I Corinthian 3:9.

During the Lord Jesus' earthly ministry, we see God the Father, the Lord Jesus, and the Holy Spirit all working together doing their part in God's plan for man. The Bible says, "But when the fulness of the time was come, God sent forth his Son, made of a woman, made under the law, To redeem them that were under the law, that we might receive the adoption of sons." Galatians 4:4-5.

Jesus Did His Part

Jesus was on a mission from God when He was in this world. He said, "I came down from heaven, not to do mine own will, but the will of him that sent me." John 6:38. He came to redeem us. He paid our sin debt in full on Calvary. The Bible says, "God commendeth his love toward us, in that, while we were yet sinners, Christ died for us." Romans 5:8. Jesus did His part. He died for our sins according to the Bible.

During His earthly mission, He began the church by the calling out of the disciples. Jesus said to them, "Follow me, and I will make you fishers of men." He also said, "I will build my church; and the gates of hell shall not prevail against it." Matthew 4:19;16:18. On this mission from God Jesus taught and trained His followers how to carry-on His mission from God. He did His part and finished His mission. On Calvary He said, "It is finished!"

Before He went back to Heaven, He said to His followers, "that they should not depart from Jerusalem, but wait for the promise of the Father, which, *saith he*, ye have heard of me. For John truly baptized with water; but ye shall be baptized with the Holy Ghost not many days hence." Acts 1:4-5.

The Holy Spirit came and did His part. The Bible says, "And when the day of Pentecost was fully come, they were all with one accord in one place. And suddenly there came a sound from heaven as of a rushing mighty wind, and it filled all the house where they were sitting. Acts 2:1-2.

God Did His Part

Here is what happened on the day of Pentecost. While Jesus was doing His part in training and teaching His followers to carry on the mission He began, God was doing His part bringing the world to Jerusalem. The Bible says, "And there were dwelling at Jerusalem Jews, devout men, out of every nation under heaven." Acts 2:5. We see at Pentecost how God the Father, and God the Son, was working together during the Lord Jesus' earthly ministry. God did His part by bring the world to Jerusalem.

God is still doing His part by bringing the world to our Jerusalem.

The Holy Spirit Did His Part

The Holy Spirit came and did His part on the day of Pentecost, by filling believers with power for their mission from God. "They were all filled with the Holy Ghost." The Bible says, "But ye shall receive power, after that the Holy Ghost is come upon you: and ye shall be witnesses unto me both in Jerusalem, and in all Judaea, and in Samaria, and unto the uttermost part of the earth." Acts 1:8. Without Him we can do nothing.

The Disciples Did Their Part

We read where the disciples did their part. The Bible says, "And they were all filled with the Holy Ghost, and began to speak with other tongues, as the Spirit gave them utterance." Acts 2:4. They told all who were in Jerusalem how to be saved. They preached the Gospel to all.

The Holy Spirit gave them power to become all God wanted them to be. The Bible says, "But as many as received him, to them gave he power to become the sons of God, *even* to them that believe on his name." John 1:12. The Bible says, "we are laborers together with God." In other words, God does His part while we do our part, and the Lord always does His part to perfection. If we understood how God works, we would have more faith concerning the mission He has given us, and we would see "the goodness of the Lord" in the lives of people.

But more importantly we would learn the importance of waiting on the Lord as He puts the circumstances together in order to change the lives of people.

An Example Of Working With God And Doing Our Part

There was a dear elderly lady in a nursing home in the county north of us who was taken to the hospital for an emergency. She was out of the nursing home where she lived for approximately ten days. To her family's distress when she was discharged from the hospital, she could not go back to the place where she had been because she lost her bed to another resident.

The closest facility she could be placed in was a nursing home in our city, miles away from her family. One can only imagine the stress and aggravation the family went through fighting with the powers that be in the healthcare industry.

To say her family was upset is putting it mildly. They did everything in their power to get her back near them. The nursing home she was put in was one in which we have regular "Gospel Hour" services. She heard our dear Brother Billy, who is one of the most Christlike men I know, preach the glorious Gospel, and he told her how to go to Heaven.

She trusted Christ as her personal Saviour and began to attend all the services we held in the facility where she was a resident. Her family continued to fight for her to be relocated to their town, but to no avail. She did her best to share with her family what the Lord had done in her life and the peace, God had given her. Sadly, she died while her family was fighting for her transfer.

We were asked to conduct her funeral service back where the family lived. At her service we shared with the family how God had brought her to our city, to live in a facility where we had a weekly "Gospel Hour," in order to know Christ as her personal Saviour.

At her funeral service, the same Gospel she had trusted was preached, and 17 family members received Christ as their personal Saviour.

We who know God and have a measure of understanding of how He works to put "All things together for good," see the big picture of how God brought her to Himself and then reached her family. We did our part, and God did His part in reaching that dear lady's family. Think about the story they can share about Gods amazing grace. We are working with God and God is working with us, "we are labourers together with God."

How can we be a better co-laborer with God?

1.Make sure you are in His family and on His team. "These things have I written unto you that believe on the name of the Son of God; that ye may know that ye have eternal life, and that ye may believe on the name of the Son of God." I John 5:13

2.Work with God His way, with His timing. "For my thoughts *are* not your thoughts, neither *are* your ways my ways, saith the LORD. For *as* the heavens are higher than the earth, so are my ways higher than your ways, and my thoughts than your thoughts." Isaiah 55:8-9

3.Find out where you fit in the work of the Lord. "For ye see your calling, brethren, how that not many wise men after the flesh, not many mighty, not many noble, *are called*:" I Corinthians 1:26

4.Let God help you to see the big picture, and His ways. "He made known his ways unto Moses, his acts unto the children of Israel." Psalm 103:7

5.Ask the Lord to open your mind of understanding. "That the God of our Lord Jesus Christ, the Father of glory, may give unto you the spirit of wisdom and revelation in the knowledge of him: The eyes of your understanding being enlightened; that ye may know what is the hope of his calling, and what the riches of the glory of his inheritance in the saints," Ephesians 1:17-19

6.Have faith in God and "believe to see the goodness of God...Have faith in God." Psalm 27:13. Mark 11:22

Building A Gospel Team

"And it came to pass afterward, that He went throughout every city and village, preaching and shewing the glad tidings of the kingdom of God: and the twelve were with Him, And certain women, which had been healed of evil spirits and infirmities, Mary called Magdalene, out of whom went seven devils, And Joanna the wife of Chuza Herod's steward, and Susanna, and many others, which ministered unto Him of their substance." Luke 8:1-3

There are three groups of people that the Lord Jesus took with Him to Galilee. He had with Him "the twelve," we will call them Leaders. He also had with Him "certain women," we will call them Workers, and He had "many others" with Him we will call them Followers.

These three groups, Leaders, Workers, and Followers represent a different level of Christian workers. On this team, there was a job for everyone, but we must remember they all "ministered unto Him." Their goal was to reach the unreached people of Galilee with the Gospel.

This pattern was used in building the workforce at Highland Park Baptist Church under Dr. Roberson's ministry. Every child of God could find their place of service in that church. Their mission was to make Christ known in their Jerusalem and around the world.

Dr. Roberson, my beloved pastor, believed the work of the Lord was not just for a chosen few, but for every believer in the pew. He put the Lord's work in the hands of the laypeople, and they filled their city with the Gospel. Allowing laypeople to serve at the highest level of leadership, in the church, was the secret of Dr. Roberson's success.

He would often say, "Trained workers are a churches greatest asset."

Leaders were on the team. "And the twelve were with Him." Luke 8:1

Every church needs leaders. The Lord Jesus has called these twelve men and now they are learning how to become leaders in God's work. There is one significant difference between a Leader, Worker, and a Follower.

A leader sees the big picture of what God is doing and accepts responsibility for what needs done. The disciples, with the exception of Judas, accepted the responsibility for getting the Gospel to the unsaved.

Dr. Roberson said often, "Everything rises and falls on leadership." This is true in our day. Leaders do not wait for others to do something; they do what needs to be done.

I have learned that the Lord will give churches all they need to accomplish the work they are willing to accept. The world is waiting for a leader in the church to see their need and by faith begin reaching them.

- They are waiting on Christians to understand that their soul is precious to God.
- They are waiting for someone who knows the Lord, to tell them how to be saved.

Workers were on the team. "And certain women, which had been healed of evil spirits and infirmities..." Luke 8:2

Workers are people who have won personal victories and want to help others come to Christ. Workers who have a heart for the work of the Lord, and who are willing to help <u>Leaders</u> do what God has put in their hearts, are priceless. A good leader will build a team of trained workers.

We can teach workers many things, but we cannot give them a heart for people. Only the Lord can do that for His children. There are two important things all workers on a church team need:

- They need a heart for people.

- They need to follow leadership.

Followers were on the team. "And many others, which ministered unto Him of their substance." Luke 8:3

Followers are people who are saved and want to reach others. They have not received all the training that a worker has received, and they do not understand the responsibility of leadership, but they have a desire to serve the Lord and have influence in the lives of others.

- Followers want to reach their family and their friends with the Gospel.
- Followers need to be encouraged by workers.

The Golden Rule in helping a Follower is to accept them where they are in their walk with Christ.

Followers will one day become workers and leaders if they are loved and helped. Followers are glad to be on the team, and they bring with them the joy of the Lord.

The Lord Jesus showed the disciples how to reach people when He allowed a Follower (the woman at the well) to be a part of His work. He encouraged all who came to Him to reach others. Followers know how to reach people.

Followers will bring their unsaved friends and loved ones to Christ if they are encouraged to do so.

A Leader accepts the responsibility for part of the work and is willing to help their pastor do what God has put in his heart to do.

A Worker loves and encourages followers and helps them reach their family and friends for Christ.

A Follower can bring more people to Jesus than a worker or a leader if helped to do so. If we use this pattern when building our team, we will see followers become workers and workers become leaders.

Church Leaders, Workers, and Followers
(Explained)

"The harvest truly is plenteous, but the labourers are few; Pray ye therefore the Lord of the harvest, that he will send forth labourers into his harvest." Matthew 9:37-38.

Leaders

A leader is someone who has given their life to do God's will. Romans12:1-2; Ephesians 5:17. Remember you can never know God's will <u>for</u> your life until you first <u>give</u> your life to do His will.

A leader is someone who has given their life to help others do what God has put in their heart to do. Nehemiah 2:12. God puts His work in the hearts of His people. If we help people do what God has put in their hearts, we are doing God's will with our life.

A leader is a believer whose life's goal is to please the Lord with their life. John 8:29. The highest goal of the Christian life is to please the Lord.

A leader is someone who is a servant to workers and followers. II Corinthians 4:5

A leader has knowledge, wisdom, and understanding in how to work with all the people God gives us. Exodus 31:3; Proverbs 2:6, 9:10; Colossians 1:9. Remember we cannot accomplish all God has given us to do if we cannot work with the people God gives us.

A leader is able to commit to teaching and train workers and followers. Matthew 28:19-20; Acts 1:1; Colossians 1:28; I Timothy 4:11; II Timothy 2:24. Remember a church's greatest asset is trained workers. It takes time to get people at a level they can help.

A leader must walk humbly. Proverbs 15:33, 18:12; Acts 20:19; I Peter 5:5

Anyone who wants the spotlight is probably not walking in the light. Proverbs 16:18

A leader must build their influence by living above reproach. I Thessalonians 5:22 Romans 14:7. Living above reproach is the only way to build influence with people.

A leader must be willing to let others receive praise and credit for a job well done without being jealous of them. I Thessalonians 1:3, 6; Philippians 1:3,7. If people never hear a "well done," they will one day quit doing what helps you to become a success.

A leader must never stop growing in faith. II Peter 3:8

A leader who stops growing will soon stop going.

Workers

Workers have won personal victories and can help others. Luke 8:1-3; Psalm 107:20. The level of our Christian service will be determined by our personal victories.

Workers want to help leaders do what God puts in their heart. Exodus 31:2, 38:22. God will always give a leader, who has accepted a work, the workers who can help him.

Workers love and accept followers. Philippians 1:3; I Thessalonians 1:8, Philemon 1:10-11

Workers need to see the worth of all people if they are going to help followers.

Workers encourage followers to reach their family and their friends. John 4:28-30; Matthew 8:16. Followers know who needs the Lord and they will bring people to Jesus.

Workers help followers find a work to do. I Corinthians 3:11; Ephesians 2:10

Workers help followers to begin serving the Lord where they are. Followers just need help getting started. Workers must believe there is a job for every child of God.

Workers understand the importance of being a Five Star Christian. Acts 2:42-47. Every victory in the Christian life is the result of doing one of these five things, and every problem in the Christian life can be traced back to the neglect of one of these five things.

Workers who are faithful will one day become leaders. I Corinthians 4:2. A faithful worker should be able to help followers to also become faithful. Proverbs 25:19

Followers

Followers have taken the first step in their newfound faith. Acts 2:41. The first step for a follower (all who have trusted Christ as their personal Saviour) is to follow the Lord in believer's baptism.

Followers have a desire to grow in the Lord. II Peter 1:5-7 Every child of God grows by adding these things.

Followers need to be taught how to be a Five Star Christin and why. Acts 2:41-47. What they are taught will make them free.

Followers want to reach their family and their friends. Mark 5:19; Luke 8:39

Followers know how to win their families to what we are doing. Remember, there are two groups of people who are difficult for us to reach. The people who think we do not like them, and the people who do not like us, both are hard for us to win. Followers help us with both groups.

"I have no sympathy with those who take hold of any kind of work with the tips of their fingers. Hold it with both hands, your success depends on it."

JPM

WHAT HAPPENED TO SUNDAY SCHOOL?

Jesus said, "Go ye therefore, and teach all nations, baptizing them in the name of the Father, and of the Son, and of the Holy Ghost: Teaching them to observe all things whatsoever I have commanded you..." Matthew 28:19-20

Strong Christians Believe In Sunday School

What ever happened to Sunday School? The strong Christians, who have gone before us, believed in the Sunday School. The great generation of Christians, who trained me, believed Sunday School is our local churches most important ministry in reaching our Jerusalem with the Gospel, and carrying on the mission Christ gave us. We must understand, "As goes the Sunday School, so grows the church."

Sunday School is the only ministry of the church where everyone from children through senior adults can find their place of service. Therefore, the goal of Sunday School should be to enlist every believer in the work of evangelizing our city and surrounding areas.

Sunday School Allows Churches To Start New Ministries

A growing Sunday School allows a church to give birth to other ministries. Churches have anchor ministries that make it possible for other ministries to function and exist. Think about a shopping mall with dozens of stores. The anchor stores are the ones making it possible for other stores to be in business. If an anchor store closes, the mall suffers.

If two anchor stores close, the mall is in trouble. If three anchor stores close, the mall is finished. It will experience a slow death.

People who are in charge must find a way to keep anchor stores strong if other stores are going to survive. We must find a way for our strongest ministry, the **Sunday School**, to live and grow if our churches are to survive.

Sunday School is the Training Ground for Workers

Sunday School is the training ground for developing workers. Jesus said, "The harvest truly is plenteous, but the labourers are few." It is in the Sunday Schools where we find workers to help advance the cause of Christ around the world. It is for this reason we say, "Trained Sunday School workers are a churches greatest asset." Sunday School members are the work force for all other church ministries. The Sunday School is the big umbrella that other church ministries work under.

Sunday School is Home Missions

Every Sunday School class should provide workers for all the ministries of their local church. Think of all the ministries, a local church could have in their Jerusalem, if the Sunday School leaders are challenged to reach everyone in their area with the Gospel. Part of the Sunday School time should be given to reporting on the progress of the church ministries, and to bring the needs of our Jerusalem missions to others. Sunday School is home missions.

Without a Sunday School we cannot reach our city. Sunday School is a network of believers working together in reaching their Jerusalem for Christ. Churches with a growing Sunday School are the only hope for our nation.

Goals for Sunday School

"As goes the Sunday School, so grows the church."

Get the Gospel to everyone in our city. "Go ye into all the world and preach the gospel to every creature." Mark 16:15

- The Gospel Challenge
- The Power Of Gospel Tracts
- Gospel Tract Routes

Baptize new believers. "Then they that gladly received his word were baptized:" Acts 2:41

- First Step In The Right Direction
- How We Identify With Jesus
- Brings Joy In A Believers Life

Work at reaching the entire family. "I have great heaviness and continual sorrow in my heart...for my brethren, my kinsmen according to the flesh:" Romans 9:2-3

"Andrew, Simon Peter's brother...first findeth his own brother Simon.... And he brought him to Jesus." John 1:40-42

- Every Child Of God's First Mission
- Learn How To Share Personal Testimony

Teach the Bible. "Teaching them to observe all things whatsoever I have commanded you:" Matthew 28:20.

- How We Teach Is Important
- What We Teach Is More Important
- How We Live Is The Most Important

Help every believer become a Five Star Christian. "And they continued stedfastly in the apostles' doctrine." Acts 2:42

- Bible
- Prayer
- Church
- Giving
- Witnessing

Train the next generation, of church members, to serve the Lord. "But continue thou in the things which thou hast learned and hast been assured of." II Timothy 3:14 "And the things that thou hast heard of me among many witnesses, the same commit thou to faithful men, who shall be able to teach others also." II Timothy 2:2

- Invest Time In Faithful Men & Women
- His Mission Is Our Mission
- Trained Workers Are The Churches Best Asset

Provide fellowship and encouragement. "If we walk in the light, as he is in the light, we have fellowship one with another." I John 1:7

- Encourage One Another
- Love One Another
- Pray For One Another

Start new ministries to reach our city. "Ye have filled Jerusalem with your doctrine." Acts 5:28

- Sunday School Classes For Every Age Group
- Sunday School Classes & Prayer Line
- Secondary Sunday Schools

Work at reaching the different language groups of people in our city. "Every man heard them speak in his own language." Acts 2:6

- The World Has Come To Our Jerusalem
- Gospel Tracts In Local Languages
- Sunday School Classes In Other Languages

Start Gospel Hours. "And they...preached the gospel in many villages of the Samaritans." Acts 8:25. "And there they preached the gospel." Acts 14:7 Gospel Hours can be started in any place where we find people:

- Gospel Hours In Nursing Homes & Assisted Living
- Gospel Hours In Mobile Home Parks
- Gospel Hours In Factories
- Gospel Clubs In Schools
- Gospel Meetings In Parks

Having a Gospel Hour ministry allows our churches to fulfill the mission Christ gave us in Acts 1:8. We can have a Gospel meeting anywhere people will gather. I can remember several men and women, who were faithful members of the Highland Park Baptist Church back in the day, reporting on services they had at the places of businesses they worked, such as factories, mills, offices, lunchrooms etc. They would tell of coworkers coming to Christ in their meetings.

Gospel Hours can be started in any place where we find people. Gospel meetings can be held in day-cares, nursing homes, schools from kindergarten through college, factories, hospitals, parks and recreation areas, resorts, and a host of a hundred other places. The door is wide open. People are waiting for us to come to them with the Gospel. We must find a way to reach our cities for Christ.

Every adult Sunday School class, including teens, needs to be involved in the Gospel Hour ministry, because of the great need for workers in this powerful ministry.

(How to start and conduct a "Gospel Hour" is covered in the **Gospel Crusader** training material.)

"You must know the Bible. It is the standard by which we examine and test the doctrines and teachings we hear."
JPM

Gospel Crusaders Verse

____**Matthew 28:19-20,** Go ye therefore, and teach all nations, baptizing them in the name of the Father, and of the Son, and of the Holy Ghost: Teaching them to observe all things whatsoever I have commanded you: and, lo, I am with you alway, even unto the end of the world. Amen.

____**Romans 3:10,23** As it is written, There is none righteous, no, not one…For all have sinned, and come short of the glory of God.

____**Romans 6:23**, For the wages of sin is death; but the gift of God is eternal life through Jesus Christ our Lord.

____**Romans 5:8**, But God commendeth His love toward us, in that, while we were yet sinners, Christ died for us.

____**Romans 10:9,** That if thou shalt confess with thy mouth the Lord Jesus, and shalt believe in thine heart that God hath raised Him from the dead, thou shalt be saved.

____**Romans 10:13**, For whosoever shall call upon the name of the Lord shall be saved.

____**Psalm 126:6,** He that goeth forth and weepeth, bearing precious seed, shall doubtless come again with rejoicing, bringing his sheaves with him.

____**I Timothy 2:5,** For there is one God, and one mediator between God and men, the man Christ Jesus.

____**John 10:27-30**, My sheep hear My voice, and I know them, and they follow Me: And I give unto them eternal life; and they shall never perish, neither shall any man pluck them out of My hand. My Father, which gave them Me, is greater than all; and no man is able to pluck them out of my Father's hand. I and my Father are one.

____**I John 5:11-12,** And this is the record, that God hath given to us eternal life, and this life is in his Son. He that hath the Son hath life; and he that hath not the Son of God hath not life.

____**John 1:11-13,** He came unto His own, and His own received him not. But as many as received Him, to them gave He power to become the sons of God, even to them that believe on His name: Which were born, not of blood, nor of the will of the flesh, nor of the will of man, but of God.

____**Matthew 4:19**, And He saith unto them, Follow Me, and I will make you fishers of men.

____**Acts 1:8**, But ye shall receive power, after that the Holy Ghost is come upon you: and ye shall be witnesses unto Me both in Jerusalem, and in all Judaea, and in Samaria, and unto the uttermost part of the earth.

____**Acts 4:31**, And when they had prayed, the place was shaken where they were assembled together; and they were all filled with the Holy Ghost, and they spake the word of God with boldness.

____**II Corinthians 5:21**, For He hath made him to be sin for us, who knew no sin; that we might be made the righteousness of God in Him.

____**Acts 4:12,** Neither is there salvation in any other: for there is none other name under heaven given among men, whereby we must be saved.

____**James 2:10**, For whosoever shall keep the whole law, and yet offend in one point, he is guilty of all.

____**John 3:18**, He that believeth on Him is not condemned: but he that believeth not is condemned already, because he hath not believed in the name of the only begotten Son of God.

____**John 3:36**, He that believeth on the Son hath everlasting life: and he that believeth not the Son shall not see life; but the wrath of God abideth on him.

____**Ephesians 2:8-9,** For by grace are ye saved through faith; and that not of yourselves: it is the gift of God: Not of works, lest any man should boast.

____**Romans 10:11**, For the scripture saith, Whosoever believeth on Him shall not be ashamed.

____**Matthew 10:32**, Whosoever therefore shall confess Me before men, him will I confess also before My Father which is in heaven.

____**Isaiah 1:18** Come now, and let us reason together, saith the LORD: though your sins be as scarlet, they shall be as white as snow; though they be red like crimson, they shall be as wool.

____**II Peter 3:9,** The Lord is not slack concerning His promise, as some men count slackness; but is longsuffering to us-ward, not willing that any should perish, but that all should come to repentance.

____**Romans 5:12,** Wherefore, as by one man sin entered into the world, and death by sin; and so death passed upon all men, for that all have sinned

____**I Peter 1:18-19,** Forasmuch as ye know that ye were not redeemed with corruptible things, as silver and gold, from your vain conversation received by tradition from your fathers; But with the precious blood of Christ, as of a lamb without blemish and without spot:

____**II Corinthians 5:17,** Therefore if any man be in Christ, he is a new creature: old things are passed away; behold, all things are become new.

____**Mark 16:15,** And He said unto them, Go ye into all the world, and preach the gospel to every creature.

____**Romans 1:16,** For I am not ashamed of the gospel of Christ: for it is the power of God unto salvation to every one that believeth; to the Jew first, and also to the Greek.

Check off each verse when put it to memory

The Gospel Award

The History of The Gospel Award
(Material repeated in this section is to help remember)

My wife and I began, what we now call, **The Gospel Award** for boys and girls in 1976. A woman in our home church was upset with the way the children, who were riding our bus to Sunday School, behaved in church. She told us we needed to teach our bus kids the Romans Road. We were both young in the Lord and had never heard of the Romans Road.

She told me that the Romans Road were verses, specifically taken from the book of Romans, that told us how to be saved and go to Heaven when we die. I asked her to write the verses down for me and we would teach our bus kids the verses.

We began by giving one verse to the children each week, with the promise that if they put that verse to memory my wife would give them a little craft item, which she had made each week. The children were excited and worked hard to put the Bible verses to memory.

My wife also encouraged our bus kids to get one of their parents to help them memorize the verses. Every week the children would get on the bus, tell her their verse, and get the little gift she had made for them that week. What the Lord did in the homes of the children, who rode our bus, still brings tears to my eyes when I think back on those early days of our ministry.

We were only in our home church, where we were saved, for a little over eleven months, but in those eleven months we saw ninety-five children and parents come to Christ.

My favorite conversion was the salvation of a widowed father named Jerry, and his four children. Jerry's wife had taken her own life one year before his four children started riding our bus to Sunday School. Jerry was a broken man because of what happened and spent his weekends at home drunk. But Jerry loved his children and allowed them to ride our bus.

His youngest daughter Monna was not yet four years old, but we let her ride our bus. She had not yet been to school and struggled with memorizing the weekly verses.

Mona had a tough time saying the verse correctly. She would give her young child translation of it. She would not say "For all have sinned and come short of the glory of God," she would say, "All have been bad, and God is mad." My wife was compassionate, and she gave her the little gift anyway.

One weekday, about eight weeks after Jerry's children had been riding our bus, when I came home from work my wife said, "Jerry called and said he got saved today." I immediately drove to Jerry's house to see him. He invited me into his house; something he had never done before.

On the coffee table, in the middle of several empty beer cans, was the verse the children had been working on that week, John 3:16. With tears of joy Jerry told me what had happened. I did not know how much Jerry loved his children and how he had been spending his evenings trying to teach Monna her Bible verses. He would go over the Bible verses with her before she went to bed.

By helping Monna learn her verses, Jerry had learned the Romans Road and had memorized John 3:16. I discovered a powerful truth about God and His Word. The Bible says, "He sent his word, and healed them, and delivered them from their destructions." Psalms 107:20. God saved Jerry, and he followed the Lord in believers' baptism. Jerry later married a sweet Christian woman and continued in his newfound faith. Little Monna grew up and became a foreign missionary.

The Gospel Award Program

Today, The Gospel Award has been developed much more fully and now uses Gospel colors to help teach God's plan of salvation. But we still get children and their parents working together in memorizing the Gospel verses.

Using colors, to teach the Gospel, was first used by a famous English preacher, Charles Haddon Spurgeon, in a message on January 11, 1866. Spurgeon was preaching to orphans who could not read. He used three colors of paper, black, red, and white to teach the glorious Gospel of Christ. He used black to represent man's sin, red to represent Christ's shed blood and death, and white to represent God's forgiveness and our new life.

This method of presenting the Gospel caught on quickly. Hudson Taylor took it to the mission field. D.L. Moody added a fourth color, gold, to represent God's love and plan for man, and used it across America in his meetings. A fifth color, green, was added to represent growing and going. Millions have been won to Christ over the years by using these colors to teach the Gospel.

The Bible teaches us that creation speaks of Gods "eternal power and Godhead." Romans 1:20. David said, "The heavens declare the glory of God...and His righteousness." Psalm 19:1. The disciples learned, from the LORD Jesus, how to use God's creation to teach the great truths about God's love and His plan for life. We use this ageless method to teach "the glorious gospel of Christ," in our Gospel Awards program.

How Does the Gospel Award Work?

The Gospel Award program helps children get assurance of their salvation and get started in their new-found faith. The program is simple enough for children to do, and yet powerful in how it transforms children and their homes and families. The children whose parents help them work on their verses become convicted of their own need of salvation.

After children have trusted Christ, as their personal Saviour, they are encouraged to work on receiving the Gospel Award. The Gospel Award is a beautiful 8x10 certificate that has the child's name and accomplishment on it.

Get Children to Sign the Pledge Card

Children will get excited about winning the Gospel Award. Show them one of the beautiful certificates framed with a child's name on it. Tell them they will receive one with their name on it and they will cherish it. Explain to them that their family and friends will be proud of their achievement and will want to see them receive their Gospel Award.

Get children to take the pledge, then they will work hard to put to memory the weekly verses. Remember, children love competition and will want to be the first one to complete the program. Let the children, in your class, share how the Lord is using them in the Gospel Award program. They will tell how the verses help them and how sharing their testimony touched a family member or friends' life. These testimonies will encourage others to do the same.

Send the Signed Pledge Card Home with the Children

The pledge card has information that will help parents understand the Gospel Award and how they can help their child achieve it. Parents are to hear their child say the verse, and tell the story of Jesus by using their Gospel color bracelet.

Parents then sign the card letting us know their child has completed the requirement to receive their award. The next step is for their child to receive their beautiful Gospel Award.

You will discover that parents want their children to learn character and have a basic knowledge of the Bible, especially verses that help them become good kids. For example, most parents do not know this great verse is in the Bible. "Children, obey your parents in the Lord: for this is right. Honour thy father and mother…That it may be well with thee, and thou mayest live long on the earth." Ephesians 6:1-3.

Most parents would love for their child to know this verse. I know my wife and I got a lot of milage out of this verse in raising our children. (-:

We present the certificates to the children in one of our morning services where parents are invited to attend, or at school assemblies where other students can be encouraged and enlisted for the next awards service. We make "Gospel Award Day," a big day in the young person's life. We have invitations that can be personalized with the child's name, using a templet, allowing each child to invite as many family members and friends as they can to their awards service.

Family members are encouraged to attend the service when their child is being honored. (I have included a lesson for your use on, "Making the Visit to Children's Home" in these lessons.)

The Gospel Award program works by getting children to do the following:

First, each week the children memorize one of the Gospel verses. We ask parents to help their children by listening to them say it and then initialing the space by the verse.

Second, once the children have memorized all the verses, we ask the parent to make sure they can tell the story of Jesus by using their Gospel bracelet and the Bible verses that they have put to memory. The Gospel bracelet can be used to share the Gospel with family members and friends. Each color is connected with a Bible verse which tells the story of Jesus and His mission from God.

Once children have shared the message of the Gospel bracelet, we ask a parent to initial the form.

Third, we help children share their faith with friends and family. Children can tell others how they came to Christ, and what He is doing in their lives. We have a Gospel tract that is used, in our children's ministry, that helps children invite their friends to church. We also teach children songs and choruses that they love to sing. We encourage them to sing these songs at home and at school knowing that God inhabits the praise of His children. (Psalm 22:3)

We encourage all our children to keep a prayer list and to pray for their family and friends. Most of the time children see results by their prayers and faithfulness. It is important that children's workers rejoice over how the Lord works in the lives of these young people.

The Gospel Bracelet

We here at Five Star Christian Ministries have designed a beautiful Gospel bracelet with five colors to be used in sharing the Gospel of Christ worldwide. After the children sign the Gospel pledge, they are given their Gospel bracelet. The bracelet has three words, "God Loves You" printed on it and the five Gospel colors that identify with the verses for each color. The Gospel bracelet helps children tell the story of Jesus and share the Gospel with their family and friends.

The Gospel bracelet is worn with the "**God Loves You**" for all to see and read. When you wear it, it is upside down to you. When you turn your wrist over the Gospel colors are in order.

Black represents our sin, **Red** represents the blood and death of Christ, **White** represents our forgiveness, and **Green** represents our Growing and Going to tell others. And of course, the **Gold** represents Gods love for all people.

This allows the one wearing the bracelet to share the Gospel with everyone they meet. Everyone who wears the Gospel bracelet should put to memory the Bible verses which go with the colors.

GOLD, God Loves You. "For God so loved the world, that he gave his only begotten Son, that whosoever believeth in him should not perish, but have everlasting life." John 3:16

BLACK, We Are All Sinners. "As it is written, There is none righteous, no, not one…For all have sinned, and come short of the glory of God." Romans 3:10,23

RED, Jesus Died for Our Sins. "But God commendeth his love toward us, in that, while we were yet sinners, Christ died for us." Romans 5:8

WHITE, Pray and Receive Forgiveness. "For whosoever shall call upon the name of the Lord shall be saved." Romans 10:13

GREEN, Grow and Go Tell Others. "Go ye into all the world and preach the gospel to every creature." Mark 16:15.

The Power of a Gospel Bracelet

The Bible says, "I am not ashamed of the gospel of Christ: for it is the power of God unto salvation to every one that believeth; to the Jew first, and also to the Greek." Romans 1:16.

Wearing a Gospel Bracelet identifies us as a follower of Christ. Jesus said, "If any man will come after me, let him deny himself, and take up his cross daily, and follow me." Luke 9:23.

Wearing a Gospel Bracelet is our testimony that we are on a mission with God. Jesus said, "As my Father hath sent me, even so send I you." John 20:21. Jesus also said, "Go ye therefore...and...I am with you alway, even unto the end of the world. Amen." Matthew 28:19-20.

Wearing a Gospel Bracelet is how we walk in the light with Jesus. The Bible says, "If we walk in the light, as he is in the light, we have fellowship one with another, and the blood of Jesus Christ his Son cleanseth us from all sin." I John 1:7. Every victory is won in His presence.

Wearing a Gospel Bracelet is how we share the Gospel and continue in the work God has given us to do. The Bible says, "Being confident of this very thing, that he which hath begun a good work in you will perform it until the day of Jesus Christ:" Philippians 1:6.

Wearing a Gospel Bracelet is how we lift Jesus up for others to see. Jesus said, "If I be lifted up from the earth, will draw all men unto me." John 12:32.

Encourage the children to faithfully wear their Gospel bracelet and hand out the five color Gospel tract. As they work on their Gospel

Award, wearing the Gospel bracelet will help them connect the colors with the verses.

Helpful Tips

- **Set a date when you will award the Gospel Award.** Children will work to complete their work if they know and understand when the big day is planned.

- **Use the chart provided** to show the progress everyone is making and be excited for them.

- **Let children share testimonies** of how the Lord is using them in giving the Gospel to their family and friends.

- **Use all the material provided by Five Star Christian Ministries** in your program. (Gospel tracts, Personal invitations, Sign-up cards, 8x10 Gospel Award, Personalized notes to parents, Gospel bracelets, Gospel pens, Charts, Commitment cards for children, devotions for children and a Salvation message outline for Gospel Award Sunday.)

- **Make sure you keep parents on board** with you helping their children learn the ABCs of Jesus, and the parents being present on Gospel Award Sunday when their child will be honored.

Making The Visit to The Home
Try To Make Sure Parents Know You Are Coming.

To get the most out of the visit, we need to plan to make it when everyone is home and when it is a good time. Set up an appointment and make sure they know that you are coming. Remember, these parents love you, and they are thankful for all that you do to help their children. They will give you this one special visit because of all that you have done for their family.

Take with you the letter from the pastor about the Gospel Award, if it has not been mailed. This letter talks about the upcoming Sunday when all the children who have earned the award will be honored in the main service. Remind them that their children will take part in the service and that there will be a place reserved for them. (More will be discussed about the service later.)

Explain To Them the Purpose of This Visit.

Begin your conversation by telling them about how thankful we are to them for allowing our church to play a part in their child's life and spiritual development.

Also, compliment them on the good job they did with helping their child learn the Bible verses. Tell them about what a great kid they have, and that they can be very proud of their child. Tell them that the reason for your visit is to make sure that everyone is all on the same page.

Rehearse With Them What Their Child Has Learned.

We let the children prepare their parents to receive Christ by getting them to earn the "Gospel Award." Remind their parents that in school children learn their ABC's and in church they learn the ABC's of Jesus. In school we get knowledge, but in church we get wisdom. Children need both knowledge and wisdom in life if they are going to be successful. Tell them that wisdom comes from knowing the Lord and His Word.

Tell them that our church recognizes young people, who know the Lord and who have put His Word to memory, by giving them the Gospel Award. Let them know that you are coming by to talk about the special service that has been planned for their child.

Review with them all their child has done to receive this special award. It is good for their son or daughter to say the Bible verses, with their parents listening, during the visit.

Often parents will say the verses with their child because they have also learned them while helping their child put them to memory.

Think about how the Lord has been working in this family. The parents have heard the Gospel, and in most cases, they have put to memory the same verses their children have learned. They have also witnessed the transformation of their children. They have listened to these powerful songs, which their children have learned, and they have seen prayers answered.

You will discover when you make the Gospel Award visit that the children have created a desire in the hearts of their parents to want to know the Lord.

Tell Them of Their Child's Decision to Receive Christ.

Tell parents that the greatest decision their child has ever made was to receive the Lord Jesus as their personal Saviour. Say for example: "_____ made a decision that he did not want to live one more day for the devil. He gave his life to the Lord, and I want you to know that I am going to do everything I can do to help and encourage him. If anyone is going to discourage him, it is not going to be me."

I like to ask children, in front of their parents, if they want to live for the devil or if they want to live for the Lord Jesus. They always say, "I want to live for Jesus." I remind the parents that I am going to always encourage their children to live for the Lord Jesus.

Give Parents an Opportunity to Receive Christ.

After we have talked to parents about their child receiving the Gospel Award, we want to pray for the family. Remember our goal is to see the entire family saved. We know that the Lord has been working in this family, and that they have heard the Gospel. Most parents will say the verses with their children from memory.

So, in our prayer we want to thank the Lord for the kindness and hospitality shown to us by this family. We also want to thank the Lord for His presence in this home and acknowledge that He desires this family to be in Heaven together.

Before we say amen to our prayer, and while heads are still bowed, ask the parents if they would be willing to receive Christ as their personal Saviour. This is a great opportunity for you to lead them in the sinner's prayer.

You will discover that after weeks of listening to their children sing about their new-found faith and helping them memorize Bible verses, that the parents are ready to be saved. Tell them that you rejoice over their decision and look forward to seeing them on Sunday.

Planning Gospel Award Sunday

Gospel Award Sunday is an exciting day for the entire church family. The boys and girls, along with the teens, have been working to receive their beautiful certificates, and many of their family members will be present.

I trust that you have read all the material provided for the workers, and that you have seen the helpful videos. If you have, then you know that a lot of work has gone into the young people, preparing their family and friends to receive the Lord Jesus as their personal Saviour.

The level of excitement about this special Sunday has been building in the children's lives. Do not mess it up by not being on the same page with the purpose of the Gospel Award Sunday. You will have unsaved parents and grandparents, along with friends of the family, at the service.

If you do not have people saved in the service, it will be because of one of two things. Number one, the Gospel has lost its power and no longer works, or number two, the Gospel is not given. In other words, give the Gospel! It will never lose its power.

How To Give an Evangelistic Invitation

There will be many unsaved people in the service on "Gospel Award" Sunday. Giving the invitation at the end of the message on this day will be different because of who is in the service. The first-time visitors on this day will have heard the testimonies of their children and will have helped them put to memory the Gospel verses. Now they have heard a simple message on God's love for people. We must give them an opportunity to receive Christ as their personal Saviour.

God says, "Come now, and let us reason together, saith the Lord: though your sins be as scarlet, they shall be as white as snow; though they be red like crimson, they shall be as wool" Isaiah 1:18. "For whosoever shall call upon the name of the Lord shall be saved" Romans 10:13.

Drawing the net and giving an evangelistic invitation is the next step after the Gospel has been given. The invitation can be given to one person, as the Lord Jesus did with Nicodemus, or to thousands, as Peter did on the day of Pentecost.

What Is Important?

It is important to make sure the Gospel has clearly been given. By that I mean we must make sure we have made the message of salvation crystal clear, on a level all people can understand. Remember, "Faith cometh by hearing, and hearing by the Word of God" Romans 10:17.

Our part is to give the Gospel, the Lord's part is to bring conviction, and the hearer's part is to believe. The Lord cannot do His part if we fail to do our part, and "How shall they believe in Him of whom they have not heard?" No wonder the Bible says, "How beautiful are the feet of them that preach the Gospel of peace, and bring glad tidings of good things!" Romans 10:14-15.

How Do We Begin The Invitation?

Once the message has been given and we have concluded have everyone bow their heads. This accomplishes two things.

One, it takes a person to another level in their thinking. The people who have heard the Gospel are now thinking about what they have heard. Two, it helps people to understand that their decision to accept or reject Christ is between them and the Lord. There will be an awareness of God's presence when you bow your head and begin praying.

It is best to say, "Let's bow our heads," before you fold papers or close your Bible. Putting away our material before we bow our heads and pray, causes people to think that we are finished. They will start thinking about leaving. We want people to think on what they have heard. We do not want them to think about what they have going on after the meeting.

Many who teach and preach the Gospel find giving the invitation very difficult. Making this transition is much easier by having people bow their heads, remain seated, and pray.

How Should We Pray?

The simplest way to begin is to say, "Let's bow our heads and pray." Begin your prayer by thanking the Lord for the opportunity that He has given people to hear the Gospel. Also ask Him to give those, who have heard the message, the courage and faith to say yes to Him.

Remember the less movement, such as having people stand up and take a song book the better. Keep the spirit of prayer. Following is a list of things that are important to mention in your prayer:

1. Thank the Lord for the kindness and the interest people have demonstrated in listening.

2. Acknowledge that the Lord has heard all that has been said and that He knows the hearts of those who have heard.

3. Thank Him for giving all who have heard a moment in their life to meet Him.

4. Ask the Lord to open their hearts and to have faith to believe.

The most important part of the invitation is the part where you lead them in the Sinner's Prayer.

Many are afraid to do this because they think that if they are led in prayer, it may not be real. However, we must remember that people, for the most part, have not been taught how to pray. People may use our words, but it is their prayer.

Remind people in your prayer, that if they would be willing to turn to Christ in repentance and faith, He will save them.

Here is a sample of a Sinner's Prayer, but remember, before you say this prayer you need to make a statement in your prayer about it. You can say, "If you want the Lord Jesus to save you today, you can pray this prayer. Here's the prayer."

The Sinner's Prayer

"Lord, I know that I am a sinner, and I believe You died and rose again for me. I trust You to forgive me. Come into my heart and save me. Help me to live for You. In Jesus' name, Amen." (You will want to say this prayer slowly in order for people to pray with you.)

After People Have Prayed

After the prayer has been given and people have prayed, have them keep their heads bowed. Find out who has trusted Christ as their personal Savior by having a show of hands. Say, "With our heads bowed, if you have invited the Lord Jesus into your heart and life, and you are not ashamed, would you raise your hand?"

Depending on the circumstances, you may wish to have them come forward. Regardless of whether or not they come forward, you need to give them some things to help them in their newfound faith. Try to get some personal information so follow-up can be made. Fill out as much of the card provided as possible. Hungry-hearted people will want to know more about the Lord Jesus and their newfound faith.

Rolling Out the Red Carpet for Parents

"Let brotherly love continue...Be not forgetful to entertain strangers..." Hebrews 13:1-3

Make parents feel welcome. Do not forget the number one reason people give for not visiting churches is, "churches are so unfriendly." This is a sad statement when we consider what a church is supposed to be. Church should be a place where everyone is welcome.

Tips to Help Gospel Award Sunday

1. Be ready for visitors. Make sure there is a place for them to park and that they have a good seat in the service. Try not to put them in the very back.

2. Make them feel welcome. Have some people ready to greet them and make them feel at home.

3. Remind them that they are our honored guests and tell them a little about the service. Let them know that the pastor is excited that they are present, and will introduce them when their child receives the Gospel Award in the service.

4. Make the presentation a big deal, in the service, and thank the parents for their love and concern for their child's spiritual well-being, training, and development. Remind the church that the children receiving this award today are great young people.

5. Move along with the service and keep it uplifting. Be brief and careful about "off the cuff" comments that unsaved people do not understand. In other words, this is not the time to talk about politics, immigrants, etc.

6. Have songs that stir the heart about salvation. Choose the songs wisely, and remember your guests know very few songs of the faith.

7. Keep the service moving. Remember there are four basic reasons unsaved people do not visit our churches:

A. Remember most unsaved people think churches are unfriendly; no one is glad to see them. Welcome people!

B. Remember most unsaved people think church services are boring, with a capital "B." Smile, be warm-hearted and keep it moving.

C. Remember most unsaved people say they have a hard time understanding what is being preached. Try to preach a message without turning to several passages. Preach the Gospel. John 3:16 will do just fine.

D. Unsaved people think there is nothing for their family at church. In other words, they do not see a need for our ministry in their family and life. Let them know all that your ministry is doing to help young people.

8. Preach a simple message of salvation. I have enclosed a simple outline on John 3:16 and a couple of outlines you can preach on Gospel Sunday.

9. Give an evangelistic invitation. To help you, I have provided one of our Gospel Crusade training lessons on the subject of "Giving an Evangelistic Invitation". I trust that it will be helpful.

10. Most importantly, record your guests. Have them fill out a visitor card with as much information as possible. Thank them, thank them, and thank them for coming and making their son or daughter's day a very special one.

Spend time with them while they are on your property and try to win them over to what you are doing for young people.

Material You Will Want to Use in your Gospel Award Program

1. Gospel bracelets to be worn by all who have part in the program.

2. Gospel Award certificates which can be personalized with our templet.

3. Pledge Cards for children to sign and take home.

4. Colored Gospel tracts for children to use.

5. Invitations children can personalize with our templets. Children can use it to invite family and friends to their award service.

6. Lessons on training workers and planning the Gospel Award service. We will include a lot of helpful material for Sunday school and church services.

7. New Steps in The Right Direction. This is a follow-up tract for all who trust Christ as their personal Savior showing them the next steps in their new-found faith.

Believe To See

"I had fainted, unless I had believed to see"
"The goodness of the Lord," and all He planned for me.

"The goodness of the Lord in the land of the living"
Can only be received by those who are believing.

Faith moves mountains into the depths of the sea.
What seems so strong crumbles to a believer on his knees.

People says show me, then I will believe.
God declares know Me, and by faith you'll see.

The world is waiting for me to "Believe to see"
It's hard to imagine, but God's best for others is up to me.

Bible Verses to Hide in Your Heart

Put God First

Matthew 6:33 "But seek ye first the kingdom of God, and his righteousness; and all these things shall be added unto you."

All Things Work Together

Romans 8:28 "And we know that all things work together for good to them that love God, to them who are the called according to his purpose."

Put the Needs of Others First

Philippians 2:20-21 "For I have no man likeminded, who will naturally care for your state. For all seek their own, not the things which are Jesus Christ's."

Encourage Someone Every Day

Hebrews 3:13 "But exhort one another daily, while it is called To day; lest any of you be hardened through the deceitfulness of sin."

Have The Mind Of The Lord

Philippians 2:5 "Let this mind be in you, which was also in Christ Jesus:"

Meditate On God's Word

Joshua 1:8 "This book of the law shall not depart out of thy mouth; but thou shalt meditate therein day and night, that thou mayest observe to do according to all that is written therein: for then thou shalt make thy way prosperous, and then thou shalt have good success."

Die To Self

John 12:24 "Verily, verily, I say unto you, Except a corn of wheat fall into the ground and die, it abideth alone: but if it die, it bringeth forth much fruit."

Be A Blessing To Others

Genesis 12:2 "And I will make of thee a great nation, and I will bless thee, and make thy name great; and thou shalt be a blessing:"

Follow Up With People

Acts 20:20 "And how I kept back nothing that was profitable unto you, but have shewed you, and have taught you publicly, and from house to house,"

Finish What You Start

Ecclesiastes 7:8 "Better is the end of a thing than the beginning thereof: and the patient in spirit is better than the proud in spirit."

Don't Look For Flaws In People

Matthew 7:3 "And why beholdest thou the mote that is in thy brother's eye, but considerest not the beam that is in thine own eye?"

Be Faithful To All Services

Hebrews 10:25 "Not forsaking the assembling of ourselves together, as the manner of some is; but exhorting one another: and so much the more, as ye see the day approaching."

Have More Faith

Mark 11:22-24 "And Jesus answering saith unto them, Have faith in God. For verily I say unto you, That whosoever shall say unto this mountain, Be thou removed, and be thou cast into the sea; and shall not doubt in his heart, but shall believe that those things which he saith shall come to pass; he shall have whatsoever he saith. Therefore I say unto you, What things soever ye desire, when ye pray, believe that ye receive them, and ye shall have them."

Be A Better Friend

Proverbs 17:17 "A friend loveth at all times, and a brother is born for adversity."

Fix Problems I Helped Start

Proverbs 16:20 "He that handleth a matter wisely shall find good: and whoso trusteth in the Lord, happy is he."

Give A Soft Answer

Proverbs 15:1 "A soft answer turneth away wrath: but grievous words stir up anger."

Live Life On The Sunny Side

I Thessalonians 5:18 "In every thing give thanks: for this is the will of God in Christ Jesus concerning you."

Mind My Own Business

1 Thessalonians 4:11 "And that ye study to be quiet, and to do your own business, and to work with your own hands, as we commanded you;"

Don't Pass The Buck

Philippians 3:8 "Yea doubtless, and I count all things but loss for the excellency of the knowledge of Christ Jesus my Lord: for whom I have suffered the loss of all things, and do count them but dung, that I may win Christ,"

Hold My Tongue

Proverbs 17:28 "Even a fool, when he holdeth his peace, is counted wise: and he that shutteth his lips is esteemed a man of understanding."

Control My Thought Life

II Corinthians 10:5 "Casting down imaginations, and every high thing that exalteth itself against the knowledge of God, and bringing into captivity every thought to the obedience of Christ;"

Move Past Failures

Philippians 3:13 "Brethren, I count not myself to have apprehended: but this one thing I do, forgetting those things which are behind, and reaching forth unto those things which are before,"

Keep My Word

Psalm 66:13-14 "I will go into thy house with burnt offerings: I will pay thee my vows, [14] Which my lips have uttered, and my mouth hath spoken, when I was in trouble."

Be Thankful

II Corinthians 9:11 "Being enriched in every thing to all bountifulness, which causeth through us thanksgiving to God."

Be Patient With People

I Thessalonians 5:14 "Now we exhort you, brethren, warn them that are unruly, comfort the feebleminded, support the weak, be patient toward all men."

Don't Be Halfhearted

Matthew 22:37 "Jesus said unto him, Thou shalt love the Lord thy God with all thy heart, and with all thy soul, and with all thy mind."

Build Believers

Jude 1:20 "But ye, beloved, building up yourselves on your most holy faith, praying in the Holy Ghost,"

Help People Go Forward

John 8:31 "Then said Jesus to those Jews which believed on him, If ye continue in my word, then are ye my disciples indeed;"

Get A Grip On The Bible

Luke 24:45 "Then opened he their understanding, that they might understand the scriptures,"

See The Big Picture

Ephesians 1:18 "The eyes of your understanding being enlightened; that ye may know what is the hope of his calling, and what the riches of the glory of his inheritance in the saints,"

Have Wisdom

James 1:5 "If any of you lack wisdom, let him ask of God, that giveth to all men liberally, and upbraideth not; and it shall be given him."

Be A Bold Witness

Acts 4:13 "Now when they saw the boldness of Peter and John, and perceived that they were unlearned and ignorant men, they marvelled; and they took knowledge of them, that they had been with Jesus."

Be All In With Jesus

Acts 20:20 "And how I kept back nothing that was profitable unto you, but have shewed you, and have taught you publicly, and from house to house,"

Reach Every Generation

Psalm 33:11 "The counsel of the Lord standeth for ever, the thoughts of his heart to all generations."

Understand The Times

I Chronicles 12:32 "And of the children of Issachar, which were men that had understanding of the times, to know what Israel ought to do; the heads of them were two hundred; and all their brethren were at their commandment."

Keep My Daily Duties

Psalm 61:8 "So will I sing praise unto thy name for ever, that I may daily perform my vows."

Walk With The Lord

Micah 6:8 "He hath shewed thee, O man, what is good; and what doth the Lord require of thee, but to do justly, and to love mercy, and to walk humbly with thy God?"

Wait On The Lord

Psalm 25:3 "Yea, let none that wait on thee be ashamed: let them be ashamed which transgress without cause."

Make Quality Decisions

Luke 10:41-42 "And Jesus answered and said unto her, Martha, Martha, thou art careful and troubled about many things: But one thing is needful: and Mary hath chosen that good part, which shall not be taken away from her. "

Pray More

I Thessalonians 5:17 "Pray without ceasing."

Strengthen Our Church

Acts 5:14 "And believers were the more added to the Lord, multitudes both of men and women."

Get Over Being Hurt

Genesis 50:20 "But as for you, ye thought evil against me; but God meant it unto good, to bring to pass, as it is this day, to save much people alive."

Start Good Habits

John 8:29 "And he that sent me is with me: the Father hath not left me alone; for I do always those things that please him."

Break Bad Habits

Romans 7:19 "For the good that I would I do not: but the evil which I would not, that I do."

Find A Job For Every Believer

I Corinthians 3:13 "Every man's work shall be made manifest: for the day shall declare it, because it shall be revealed by fire; and the fire shall try every man's work of what sort it is."

Be A Practicing Christian

Philippians 1:21 "For to me to live is Christ, and to die is gain."

Help People See Their Calling

I Corinthians 1:26 "For ye see your calling, brethren, how that not many wise men after the flesh, not many mighty, not many noble, are called."

Keep Myself In Shape

I Corinthians 9:27 "But I keep under my body, and bring it into subjection: lest that by any means, when I have preached to others, I myself should be a castaway."

Turn People Toward Leadership

I Thessalonians 1:6 "And ye became followers of us, and of the Lord, having received the word in much affliction, with joy of the Holy Ghost."

Reach My Family

Romans 9:2-3 "That I have great heaviness and continual sorrow in my heart. [3] For I could wish that myself were accursed from Christ for my brethren, my kinsmen according to the flesh:"

Have A Clean Heart

Hebrews 9:14 "How much more shall the blood of Christ, who through the eternal Spirit offered himself without spot to God, purge your conscience from dead works to serve the living God?"

Stay On Track With My Life

Hebrews 12:1-2 "Wherefore seeing we also are compassed about with so great a cloud of witnesses, let us lay aside every weight, and the sin which doth so easily beset us, and let us run with patience the race that is set before us, [2] Looking unto Jesus the author and finisher of our faith; who for the joy that was set before him endured the cross, despising the shame, and is set down at the right hand of the throne of God."

Stay Excited About The Lords Work

Colossians 3:23 "And whatsoever ye do, do it heartily, as to the Lord, and not unto men."

Invest The Influence Of Others

Philippians 2:16 "Holding forth the word of life; that I may rejoice in the day of Christ, that I have not run in vain, neither laboured in vain."

Start A Work For God

Philippians 1:6 "Being confident of this very thing, that he which hath begun a good work in you will perform it until the day of Jesus Christ."

Be A Doer Not A Hearer

James 1:22 "But be ye doers of the word, and not hearers only, deceiving your own selves."

Keep My Eyes On JESUS

Hebrews 12:2 "Looking unto Jesus the author and finisher of our faith; who for the joy that was set before him endured the cross, despising the shame, and is set down at the right hand of the throne of God."

Lighten Up

Hebrews 12:1 "Wherefore seeing we also are compassed about with so great a cloud of witnesses, let us lay aside every weight, and the sin which doth so easily beset us, and let us run with patience the race that is set before us,"

Number My Days

Psalm 90:12 "So teach us to number our days, that we may apply our hearts unto wisdom."

Buy Heavens Gold

Revelation 3:18 "I counsel thee to buy of me gold tried in the fire, that thou mayest be rich; and white raiment, that thou mayest be clothed, and that the shame of thy nakedness do not appear; and anoint thine eyes with eyesalve, that thou mayest see."

Hide The Word of God In My Heart

Psalm 119:11 "Thy word have I hid in mine heart, that I might not sin against thee."

Invest In People

II Timothy 2:2 "And the things that thou hast heard of me among many witnesses, the same commit thou to faithful men, who shall be able to teach others also."

Stand Up For Jesus

Ephesians 6:13-14 "Wherefore take unto you the whole armour of God, that ye may be able to withstand in the evil day, and having done all, to stand. [14] Stand therefore, having your loins girt about with truth, and having on the breastplate of righteousness;"

Be Faithful

1 Corinthians 4:2 "Moreover it is required in stewards, that a man be found faithful."

Be Good Ground For God

Mark 4:20 "And these are they which are sown on good ground; such as hear the word, and receive it, and bring forth fruit, some thirtyfold, some sixty, and some an hundred."

Love The People God Has Given Me

Philippians 1:7 "Even as it is meet for me to think this of you all, because I have you in my heart; inasmuch as both in my bonds, and in the defence and confirmation of the gospel, ye all are partakers of my grace."

Help The Women Who Serve

Philippians 4:3 "And I intreat thee also, true yokefellow, help those women which laboured with me in the gospel, with Clement also, and with other my fellowlabourers, whose names are in the book of life."

Study Great Truths of the Bible

II Timothy 2:15 "Study to shew thyself approved unto God, a workman that needeth not to be ashamed, rightly dividing the word of truth."

Continue to Make New Friends

Proverbs 18:24 "A man that hath friends must shew himself friendly: and there is a friend that sticketh closer than a brother."

Be A Team Player

I Corinthians 3:9 "For we are labourers together with God: ye are God's husbandry, ye are God's building."

Ignore My Critics

II Timothy 4:14-15 "Alexander the coppersmith did me much evil: the Lord reward him according to his works: Of whom be thou ware also; for he hath greatly withstood our words."

Get Over My Foraker's

II Timothy 4:10 "For Demas hath forsaken me, having loved this present world, and is departed unto Thessalonica; Crescens to Galatia, Titus unto Dalmatia."

Go Through The Door God Opens

I Corinthians 16:9 "For a great door and effectual is opened unto me, and there are many adversaries."

Walk With The Wise

Proverbs 13:20 "He that walketh with wise men shall be wise: but a companion of fools shall be destroyed."

Encourage Myself In The Lord

I Samuel 30:6 "And David was greatly distressed; for the people spake of stoning him, because the soul of all the people was grieved, every man for his sons and for his daughters: but David encouraged himself in the Lord his God."

Build My Influence

Romans 14:7 "For none of us liveth to himself, and no man dieth to himself."

Stand In My Place

Judges 7:21 "And they stood every man in his place round about the camp: and all the host ran, and cried, and fled."

Control My Anger

Ephesians 4:26 "Be ye angry, and sin not: let not the sun go down upon your wrath:"

See The Positive In Life

Exodus 14:31 "And Israel saw that great work which the Lord did upon the Egyptians: and the people feared the Lord, and believed the Lord, and his servant Moses."

Be Kind To Others

Romans 12:10 "Be kindly affectioned one to another with brotherly love; in honour preferring one another;"

Be A Vessel For God To Use

II Timothy 2:21 "If a man therefore purge himself from these, he shall be a vessel unto honour, sanctified, and meet for the master's use, and prepared unto every good work."

Pray For Our Leaders

I Timothy 2:1-3 "I exhort therefore, that, first of all, supplications, prayers, intercessions, and giving of thanks, be made for all men; [2] For kings, and for all that are in authority; that we may lead a quiet and peaceable life in all godliness and honesty. [3] For this is good and acceptable in the sight of God our Saviour;"

Take Time To Enjoy Life

I Timothy 6:7 "For we brought nothing into this world, and it is certain we can carry nothing out."

Pray for the Peace of Jerusalem

Psalm 122:6 "Pray for the peace of Jerusalem: they shall prosper that love thee.

Believe To Believe

I John 5:13 "These things have I written unto you that believe...that ye may believe ...."

Understand The Devil Really Wants Me

Luke 22:31 "And the Lord said, Simon, Simon, behold, Satan hath desired to have you, that he may sift you as wheat"

Give My Life To Do God's Will

Ephesians 5:17 "Wherefore be ye not unwise, but understanding what the will of the Lord is."

It's My Move

James 4:8 "Draw nigh to God, and he will draw nigh to you. Cleanse your hands, ye sinners; and purify your hearts, ye double minded."

IADOM (It All Depends On Me)

John 15:7 "If ye abide in Me, and My words abide in you, ye shall ask what ye will, and it shall be done unto you."

The Goal Of My Life

John 8:29 "And he that sent me is with me: the Father hath not left me alone; for I do always those things that please him."

Do My Part

Proverbs 3:5-6 "Trust in the LORD with all thine heart; and lean not unto thine own understanding. In all thy ways acknowledge Him, and He shall direct thy paths."

Continue

II Timothy 3:14 "But continue thou in the things which thou hast learned and hast been assured of, knowing of whom thou hast learned them"

God Is For Me

Psalm 56:9 "...This I know...God is for me."

The Best Is Yet To Come

I Corinthians 3:21-23 "...For all things are yours...the world, or life, or death, or things present, or things to come; all are yours..."

Walk In The Light

I John 1:7 "But if we walk in the light, as He is in the light, we have fellowship one with another, and the blood of Jesus Christ his Son cleanseth us from all sin."

They Are Not Giants And I Am Not A Grasshopper

Numbers 13:33 "And there we saw the giants, the sons of Anak, which come of the giants: and we were in our own sight as grasshoppers, and so we were in their sight."

Everything Rises And Falls On Leadership

I Corinthians 11:1 "Be ye followers of me, even as I also am of Christ."

Bear One Another's Burdens

Galatians 6:2 "Bear ye one another's burdens, and so fulfil the law of Christ."

Having One Of Those Days

Luke 20:1 "...One of those days..."

Build Memories

Philippians 1:3 "I thank my God upon every remembrance of you."

Remember Our Appointment With Jesus

II Corinthians 5:10 "For we must all appear before the judgment seat of Christ; that every one may receive the things done in his body, according to that he hath done, whether it be good or bad."

Remember The Poor

Galatians 2:10 "Only they would that we should remember the poor; the same which I also was forward to do."

Reach Children

Mark 10:14-15 "Jesus...said unto them, Suffer the little children to come unto me, and forbid them not: for of such is the kingdom of God...Whosoever shall not receive the kingdom of God as a little child, he shall not enter therein."

Live Without Fear

II Timothy 1:7 "For God hath not given us the spirit of fear; but of power, and of love, and of a sound mind."

Be On Time

Daniel 11:29 "At the time appointed he shall return, and come toward the south; but it shall not be as the former, or as the latter."

www.ingramcontent.com/pod-product-compliance
Lightning Source LLC
Chambersburg PA
CBHW050443150626
46551CB00028B/1227